Sunset
Food
Processor
Cook Book

By the Editors of Sunset Books and Sunset Magazine

Lane Publishing Co. • Menlo Park, California

Food Processor Cooking — Sophisticated or Simple

The food processor is an amazing machine that makes even the most difficult cooking job easier. It is impartial—it saves preparation time for *haute cuisine* as readily as it does for family meals; it will chop an onion for pâté as quickly as for pizza. It shreds cheese for quiche or carrots for carrot cake, slices cabbage for slaw or cucumbers for pickles, blends dough for pasta or for pastry. Whether you cook because you love to, or cook because you must, the food processor will bring you more pleasure in the kitchen.

In this book we've taken the mystery out of food processors. If you are a new owner, you'll benefit from our step-by-step directions on processor techniques. And whether you have had your machine for a week or for several years, you'll value the dozens of tempting, timesaving recipes designed for the processor to do much of the work.

We wish to express our appreciation to Ellen Fujioka who enthusiastically discovered the skills of the many machines used in our recipe testing.

Edited by Janeth Johnson Nix

Special Consultant: Kandace Esplund Reeves

Design: Steve Reinisch

Photography: Tom Wyatt
            with Lynne B. Morrall

Illustrations: Dick Cole

Covers: Tomato pizza (page 48) is our front cover subject; back cover shows fresh fruit ices (page 70). Photographs by Tom Wyatt.

Editor, Sunset Books: David E. Clark

Fourth Printing June 1980

Contents

Special Features

Introducing the Food Processor

Unveiling the secrets of your versatile machine

Whether you cook because you love to, or cook because you must, a food processor makes the job faster and more enjoyable.

The amount of time you spend in your kitchen and the kinds of food you cook are very personal things. You may find great satisfaction and pleasure in adding to your cooking repertoire — trying out new recipes, experimenting with unusual foods, or making things from scratch. On the other hand, you may be the cook on the run — the one who gets in and out of the kitchen in a hurry. Or, like many of us, you may serve quick meals during the week and enjoy the leisure of weekends to exercise your culinary talents.

This book is about using a food processor to prepare delicious food in the shortest possible time. If you have never used a food processor, the next few pages are intended for you. If you already own a food processor and know it well, you may prefer to turn directly to the recipes.

The Machine—A Talented Assistant

A food processor is a compact, portable unit that chops, purées, blends, mixes, kneads, grates, slices, and shreds. It is only slightly larger than a blender, simple to operate, and a breeze to clean; best of all, it works with incredible speed.

Surprisingly, the machine consists of few parts—a power base, work bowl, work bowl cover and feed tube, food pusher, and three or four changeable blades. By changing blades, you can use a food processor to prepare all types of food—from pizza to pâté, coleslaw to croissants, herb butters to brioches, vichyssoise to velvety mousse, cheese balls to cioppino, soups to sauces, dips to desserts, and more.

The food processor will handle small amounts of food (baby food for one or beef tartare for two) as easily as larger amounts (minestrone for 12), and it produces gourmet cooking and back-to-basics cooking with equal success. As you work with your own food processor and read this book, you'll make your own discoveries about the versatility of the machine.

This is not to say that the food processor replaces every other piece of equipment in the kitchen. It is not designed to whip air into ingredients such as egg whites and cream; the processor blade turns so rapidly that it breaks down the air bubbles almost as soon as they form, resulting in a dense, low-volume whipped product. The machine does not grind coffee or grain, extract juice, or handle large quantities of heavy dough.

Nor does the food processor completely eliminate the use of a knife. When you want perfectly cut vegetables such as julienne (matchstick pieces), miniature cubes, or roll-cut or diagonal slices (called for in Oriental cooking), or when you want symmetrical slices of fruits or vegetables to serve as a garnish, you need to cut by hand. But what a food processor does, it does exceedingly well, and day in and day out it will relieve you of many of the tedious and time-consuming jobs of food preparation.

You Have a Choice of Brands

Available on today's market are many brands of food processors having the same basic design. All of them come with at least three standard attachments—a metal blade (for chopping), a slicing disc, and a shredding disc. Processors differ in the way the power is supplied (direct drive or belt driven), the capacity of the work bowl, the absence or presence of a handle on the work bowl, the size of the feed tube, the manner in which the on-off action is controlled (by a switch or by rotating the cover of the work bowl), the noise level, and the number of special attachments available. Before buying a processor, ask to see it in action (most stores will give a demonstration) and look over the instruction manual to see what limits, if any, the manufacturer sets on its particular machine.

Make It a Habit

The investment in a food processor (from under $100 to over $200) is considerable, and it may seem excessive if you don't use the machine on a frequent basis. A good way to make certain you use it is to make a permanent place for it on your counter — although a food processor is portable, you won't use it often if you have to take it out of a cupboard each time.

Old habits are hard to break. As a new owner of a food processor, you may need to retrain yourself if you're to use it to its fullest capacity. Each time you begin food preparation, ask yourself if you could

relegate the job to the machine. If you want to slice one small onion to garnish a hamburger, it probably would be simpler to do it with a knife. But if you want to chop an onion as well as several other ingredients for spaghetti sauce, the food processor

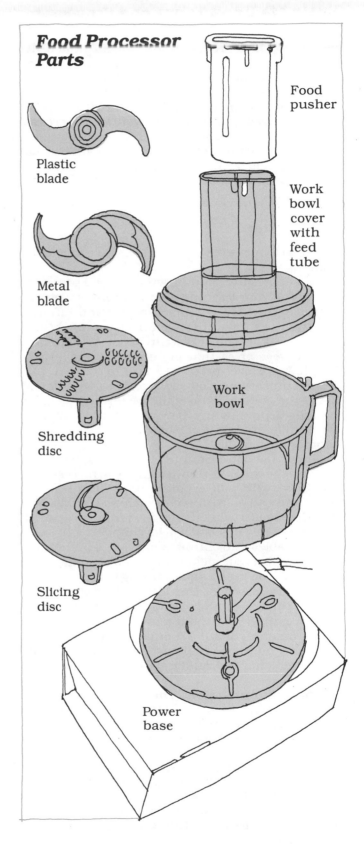

Food Processor Parts

Food pusher

Plastic blade

Metal blade

Work bowl cover with feed tube

Shredding disc

Work bowl

Slicing disc

Power base

could do it in half the time. The more you use it, the more you will find ways to make a food processor work for you.

Getting to Know Your Food Processor

Operating a food processor is simple. But don't let this fact lull you into ignoring the instruction manual. *It is absolutely essential that anyone using the machine read the instruction manual thoroughly and become familiar with all the parts before connecting and operating a food processor for the first time.* Specific operating instructions vary slightly with each brand; your instruction manual should be the final word on the capabilities of your particular machine.

How to Chop

The metal blade is the master tool; you use it for all chopping.

Your success in chopping with the food processor depends on your learning about timing, which you control by turning the machine on and off. It is important to think "off" as soon as you think "on." Many times a second or two can make the difference between vegetables that are chopped and vegetables that are over-processed and watery. At any point in processing, you can stop the machine and look at the texture. This is the easiest way to judge how long to process any item, and after you process several different kinds of food, your sense of timing becomes automatic.

In order to chop food into even pieces, you must first load the work bowl with fairly even pieces—you can't start with half a potato and a few slices of potato and end up with evenly chopped potato. As a rule, the smaller you cut the food to be processed, the more evenly the food will be chopped. Cut fruits and vegetables into chunks roughly 1½ inches on a side or smaller; cut meat into 1-inch chunks. You'll save time if you keep a small cutting board and knife near the processor for this initial chunking.

When you are chopping large amounts of food in the processor, you'll find it more efficient to do it in several batches, about 1½ cups at a time. It takes only a second to empty the work bowl of the chopped ingredients and refill it with another portion.

Practice with an onion. The first time you use a food processor, you may end up processing a dozen things from your refrigerator. The machine is fascinating to use, and once you begin experimenting, it's difficult to stop — this may prove to be a good time to serve vegetable salad.

If you feel hesitant because the machine works so quickly, try this. Set the empty work bowl, without the blade, on the power base, put on the cover, and practice turning the machine on and off. Do it again

CUT VEGETABLES *in chunks before processing with metal blade; this ensures evenly chopped food.*

quickly, on-off, on-off. The action will not harm the machine. This method, using short bursts of power, gives you fine control.

Now cut an onion into 1½-inch chunks. Fit the metal blade in the work bowl, add the onion, replace the cover, and give the machine three on-off bursts. What happens takes place so rapidly you won't be able to watch, but each time you turn the motor off, the food drops to the bottom of the work bowl so it will be in the path of the blade when the motor is restarted. Thanks to this on-off technique, all of the food in the work bowl will be evenly chopped.

Lift the cover and look at the onion. It will be coarsely chopped. Apply two or three more on-off bursts and the onion will be finely chopped — by hand, it would have been a teary, time-consuming job. If you can't resist the temptation to continue processing, in seconds the onion will end up as purée. If you originally planned to purée the onion, you would process it for about 5 seconds without turning the motor on and off.

Different methods for different foods. You use the technique of on-off bursts to chop foods that have a fairly high water content — vegetables such as celery, green onions, green peppers, mushrooms, onions, potatoes, spinach, tomatoes, and zucchini, as well as fruits, nuts, hard-cooked eggs, raw meat, and cooked meat.

To coarsely chop firm foods such as raw carrots and turnips, salami, cooked bacon, or coconut, turn the motor on and off with 3-second bursts. To finely chop firm foods, turn the motor on and process continuously until the food reaches the finely chopped stage.

For perfectly chopped parsley, remove the stems and process the feathery sprigs continuously until they are finely chopped. But be sure the parsley is dry; wet parsley turns to mush.

Because each food has its own texture, it also has

its own individual processing time. If you planned to chop two dissimilar vegetables—such as carrots, which are hard, and onions, which are watery—you would do one of two things: either process them separately, or process the carrot until it was partially chopped, then add the onion near the end of the processing time. This technique also comes into play when a recipe calls for garlic and onion. Process the garlic first (drop it down the feed tube while the motor is running), then turn the motor off, add the onion, and process with on-off bursts until the onion is chopped. This way, the garlic will be finely chopped but the onion will not become overchopped.

Some kinds of chopping call for turning the motor on and dropping pieces of food down the feed tube while the blade is rotating. This is the way to make crumbs from crackers or dried bread. Break the crackers in pieces that will fit in the feed tube and add them a few at a time, continuing to process until the total mixture is crumbed. Cup the palm of your hand lightly over the top of the feed tube to hold back small flying crumbs. If you were to start the machine with the cracker pieces in the work bowl, a piece might become wedged between the processor bowl and blade. This would not damage the machine, but removing the work bowl and looking for the offending piece would be an inconvenience.

How to Purée

You use the metal blade to purée food. Though this technique is a continuation of chopping, you do not use the on-off burst principle. Turn the machine on and process until the mixture is smooth.

You can do this to make dips, soups, pâtés, and fruit and vegetable purées. Purée meat in 2-cup portions or less. For thick soups and for fruit and vegetable purées, limit each batch to 3 cups.

The processor is more efficient at puréeing thick mixtures than thin ones. For the smoothest soup, process the cooked vegetables first before combining them with liquid. Because a food processor bowl is made of a tough, heat-resistant material, there is no need to let hot food become cool before puréeing it.

How to Blend and Mix

The food processor is perfect for mixing a wide range of foods, from crêpe batter to dips or cooky doughs to cake batters. It will combine cold butter, shortening, or cheese with flour or sugar, and it will emulsify sauces such as mayonnaise. The metal blade is the major tool for mixing.

When working with liquids or thin batters, keep in mind the capacity of the work bowl in order to avoid overflows. Processor brands vary, but as a rule of thumb, a work bowl will handle up to 2 cups of thin liquid and up to 4 cups of thick batter. Remember, too, when working with liquids and batters, to remove the processor bowl from the base as soon as you finish processing. This allows the metal blade to settle on the bottom of the work bowl, forming an almost perfect seal.

When you want to cream butter or margarine, it is not necessary to let it come to room temperature first. Cut it in ½-inch chunks or ¼-inch-thick slices and process with the metal blade until soft. If you need to cream a large quantity, turn the processor on and drop the pieces down the feed tube a few at a

ADD LIQUID through feed tube with processor turned on when you make sauce, pasta, or pastry.

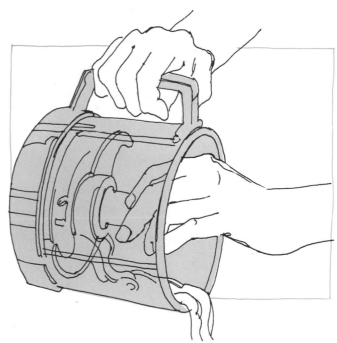

HOLD METAL BLADE in place when you pour out liquids; otherwise blade will fall out.

time. You can use the same technique with cream cheese.

In some cases, especially when working with pastry, the butter or other fat must be frozen. By using on-off bursts, you can cut the fat into the flour (necessary to produce flakiness) and be sure that the mixture will not be creamed.

How to Slice

The slicing disc will slice fruit as soft as bananas and vegetables as hard as carrots. It will also slice firm meat such as salami, and firm cheese such as mozzarella, jack, provolone, and Swiss. Check your manufacturer's recommendation for slicing cooked and raw meat.

With any fruit or vegetable, the trick to making neat slices is to cut the food in pieces to fit snugly in the feed tube (lengths for carrots and celery, wedges for cabbage and lettuce, halves for green peppers and fat onions). Arrange the food vertically or horizontally in the feed tube, packing it so it fits well but not too tightly. Stand the food pusher on top of the food, press down on the food pusher, and turn on the machine. Presto, the job is done. The harder you press down on the food pusher (keep a light touch with soft foods), the thicker the slices. Press gently for thinner slices.

As the food swooshes down the feed tube and comes in contact with the whirling slicing disc, a piece may fall over on its side, resulting in a few uneven slices. To help prevent this, load the feed tube snugly and press down on the food pusher without hesitation after you turn on the machine. Every single slice may not look picture perfect in the processor bowl, but in most cases you won't notice it in the finished dish.

FILL FEED TUBE with vegetables cut to fit; press down with food pusher for slicing or shredding.

How to Shred

The technique for shredding is similar to the one for slicing. Use the shredding disc, cut the food in pieces to fit the feed tube, and push down firmly on the food pusher. You can shred vegetables (carrots for carrot cake or a quick sautéed vegetable, potatoes for potato pancakes, cabbage for slaw), fruits, and firm cheese such as jack, Swiss, or Cheddar. To grate hard cheese, see page 58.

When you shred carrots or other firm vegetables, you may find an end piece on top of the shredding disc after you remove the work bowl cover. Don't think your machine is poorly designed—remember what happens when you shred a carrot by hand? Most of us eat the end piece without thinking about it.

Processor Safety and Convenience

A food processor is designed for both safety and efficiency, and there are rules of common sense you must follow for safe, trouble-free, effective service from the machine.

● Handle the metal blade and discs with as much respect as you would a knife. The cutting edges are razor sharp.

● *Never* insert any blade until work bowl is locked into place. After inserting a blade or disc, be sure that it is down as far as it can go on the motor shaft.

● *Always* use the food pusher when slicing or shredding. *Never* put your fingers in the feed tube.

● Avoid moving parts. *Always* wait for the metal blade or a disc to stop spinning before you remove the cover.

● When chopping food, insert the metal blade before adding food to the work bowl. This is easy to forget at first. It will not cause any damage, but it is a nuisance to empty the contents of the work bowl, fit in the blade, and start again.

● To empty the work bowl filled with dry ingredients, remove the blade first or hold the blade in place with your fingers as you tip the bowl upside down.

● To empty the work bowl filled with liquid, hold the blade in place against the bottom of the bowl with a spatula or your hand. This prevents leakage and eliminates the possibility of the blade dropping out and cutting your finger.

● Never soak the metal blade in a pan of soapy water and plan to wash it later. You may forget about it and be unable to see the sharp edges through the suds when you return. The easiest way to wash the metal blade is to scrub it with a stiff brush.

● A food processor is built with a temperature-controlled circuit breaker that automatically cuts off the current if a machine overheats from mixing a too-heavy load. If your machine stops, turn off the motor, then wait the length of time recommended in your manual before starting the machine again.

Processor-styled Recipes

Since we would like all food processor owners to be able to use this book, we have included only recipes that require the standard attachments.

As part of the initial research for this book, we interviewed dozens of men and women who owned food processors to find out what kind of information would help them use a processor in all aspects of cooking. We found a consensus that once you learn processor techniques, you do not need to learn an entire new school of cooking to work with the machine. However, to make the most of a processor's capabilities and to eliminate continual washing of the bowl and blades, you need to look at a recipe in a nonconventional way.

The recipes in this book were tested with a variety of brands of food processors and written in a style for food processor use. As you read these recipes

and cook, think about ways you can convert your own favorite recipes to a food processor style.

For example, if you planned to make an apple pie with a crumb topping, you would process the topping first because it is the driest mixture. After emptying the processor bowl, you would, without washing the bowl and blade, prepare the pastry. Then you would switch to the slicing blade and — again without washing the parts — slice the apples.

If a soup recipe called for chopped parsley as both an ingredient and a garnish, you would process all the parsley at one time and set part of it aside for the final assembly.

If you were making cookies with nuts, you would process the nuts first (while the bowl was dry), set them aside, then prepare the buttery cooky dough.

Often, there is no right or wrong order for processing foods, but if you think through a recipe before you begin to cook, you will be able to keep cleanup time to a minimum.

Food Processor Food Conversion Table

Food	Amount	Yield	Food	Amount	Yield
Bread			**Meat & Poultry**		
Crisp dried	1 sandwich-size slice	¼ cup fine crumbs	Cooked or uncooked	½ pound boneless meat	1 cup chopped meat
Fresh	1 sandwich-size slice	½ cup soft crumbs	**Vegetables**		
			Cabbage	1 medium-size (1½ lbs.)	4 cups shredded 4 cups sliced
Crackers			Carrot	1 medium-size	½ cup coarsely chopped ½ cup sliced ½ cup shredded
Graham	16 squares	1 cup crumbs			
Saltine	28 squares	1 cup crumbs			
Vanilla wafers	24 cookies (2-inch)	1 cup crumbs	Celery	1 large stalk	⅔ cup coarsely chopped ½ cup finely chopped ⅔ cup sliced
Zweiback	13 pieces	1 cup crumbs			
			Cucumber	1 large	1 cup coarsely chopped 1½ cups sliced
Cheese					
Jack, Swiss, Cheddar, or any other firm cheese	4 ounces	1 cup shredded	Green pepper	1 medium-size	¾ cup coarsely chopped ¾ cup sliced
			Mushrooms	½ pound	1½ cups sliced 1½ cups coarsely chopped
Parmesan, asiago, or any other hard cheese	3 ounces	½ cup finely chopped	Onion	1 medium-size	½ cup coarsely chopped ½ cup sliced
Fruit			Parsley	½ cup packed parsley sprigs	¼ cup finely chopped
Apple	1 medium-size	½ cup coarsely chopped ¾ cup shredded ½ to ⅔ cup sliced	Potato	1 medium-size	¾ cup coarsely chopped 1 cup shredded ¾ cup sliced
Banana	1 medium-size	1 cup sliced			
Pear	1 medium-size	½ cup coarsely chopped	Zucchini	1 medium-size	1 cup coarsely chopped 1 cup sliced
Pineapple	1 medium-size	4 cups sliced			

Appetizers & First Courses

From spur-of-the moment dips and hot hors d'oeuvres to glorious pâtés and terrines, this chapter samples some of the good things you can prepare with a food processor. It may come as a surprise that many dishes usually considered too complicated or time consuming to prepare at home can be made easily with a food processor. Once you learn the techniques of chopping, slicing, mixing, and puréeing, you can prepare any dish, from the simplest to the most sophisticated.

Freezer Cheese Balls

(Pictured on page 18)

Your freezer can be your ally when you make these cheese balls ahead for a party.

> 8 ounces sharp Cheddar cheese
> 1 clove garlic
> 1 large package (8 oz.) cream cheese or
>   Neufchâtel cheese
> 4 ounces blue cheese
> ¼ cup butter or margarine
> ¾ cup walnuts or pecans
>   Crackers or Melba toast

Use shredding disc to shred Cheddar cheese; set cheese aside. Change to metal blade and process garlic until chopped. Cut cream cheese, blue cheese, and butter into chunks. With processor running, drop chunks down feed tube and process until smooth. Add shredded cheese and process until mixture is creamy.

Cover and chill cheese mixture for about 3 hours or until firm enough to shape. Divide mixture in half and shape each half into a smooth ball; wrap airtight in clear plastic wrap, place in plastic bag, and refrigerate or freeze.

To serve, let frozen cheese balls stand at room temperature, unwrapped, 3 or 4 hours. Using the metal blade, process nuts until coarsely chopped. Roll each ball in nuts, pressing in lightly. Serve with assorted crackers or wafers. Makes 2 balls, each about 3 inches in diameter.

Fila Cheese Onion Rolls

(Pictured on page 18)

Similar in flavor to an onion quiche, this appetizer is faster to prepare for a crowd. Look for the ready-made fila dough in delicatessens or in the frozen food section of large markets. It won't matter if the thin layers or sheets of fila tear a bit as you separate them, but keep the dough covered with clear plastic wrap except when actually working with each layer. Otherwise, the dough will dry out and become brittle.

> 3 large onions
> ½ cup (¼ lb.) butter or margarine
> 6 ounces Gruyère, Samsoe, Swiss, or
>   jack cheese
> 2 small packages (3 oz. *each*) cream cheese
> ½ teaspoon caraway seed (optional)
> 9 to 12 sheets of fila, *each* about 16 by 24
>   inches (about ½ lb.)

Insert slicing disc in food processor. Cut onions in quarters to fit feed tube and slice. Melt 3 tablespoons of the butter in a wide frying pan; add onion and cook over moderate heat, stirring frequently, for 20 minutes or until onion is limp and pale gold, but not browned, and most of liquid has evaporated. Cool to lukewarm.

Change to shredding disc and shred Gruyère cheese; transfer to a bowl. Change to metal blade; cut cream cheese in chunks, process until soft, and add to shredded cheese along with caraway seed and cooked onion; stir to mix well. Melt remaining 5 tablespoons butter in a small pan.

To make each roll, stack 3 or 4 sheets of fila horizontally and brush very lightly between sheets with some of the butter (streak in a few places, don't coat the whole sheet). Then spoon on ⅓ of cheese-onion mixture in an even band along one long edge of fila and roll to enclose. Cut roll in half and place halves, seam side down, on a baking sheet; brush entire surface of rolls well with butter to prevent drying. Repeat, making 2 more rolls. (At this point you can cover rolls with clear plastic wrap and refrigerate until next day.)

Just before baking, cut rolls on pan in 1-inch pieces and leave slices standing in place. Bake, uncovered, in a 400° oven for about 12 minutes (about 17 minutes if chilled) or until golden brown. Let cool slightly so cheese will solidify; then serve. Makes about 4 dozen appetizers.

Cheese Crock

Once you start the cheese crock you can add remnants of almost any firm cheese and keep a cheese mixture going indefinitely. Before serving, let the cheese soften at room temperature or, if time is short, reprocess a portion to soften it.

- 1 pound sharp Cheddar cheese
- 1 small package (3 oz.) cream cheese
- 1½ tablespoons olive oil or salad oil
- 1 teaspoon *each* dry mustard and garlic salt
- 2 tablespoons brandy

Use shredding disc to shred Cheddar cheese; set cheese aside. Change to metal blade. Cut cream cheese in chunks and process until smooth. Add shredded cheese, oil, mustard, garlic salt, and brandy and process until well blended. Pack into a container, cover, and refrigerate for about a week before using for the first time. Makes about 3 cups.

Adding to the crock. Firm cheeses — such as **Swiss,** jack, or any Cheddar types—are fine. Shred cheese, then use metal blade to process it together with cheese from crock. Process mixture until smooth, adding small amounts of **oil** or cream cheese for good consistency. Also add **brandy,** dry sherry, port, beer, or kirsch, in same proportion as original amount of brandy. Then let mixture age a few days before serving. Use it every week or two, saving part of original mixture to keep the crock going.

Vegetable-based Dips

(Creamy Spinach Dip pictured on page 18)

It's hard to imagine a lighter or more refreshing appetizer than vegetables dipped in a vegetable-based sauce. Serve the following two dips separately or together, for they both complement the same fresh, raw vegetables. Arrange the vegetable dippers attractively in a basket. Carrot, celery, and zucchini strips; pieces of broccoli and cauliflower; and radishes and cherry tomatoes are all good. For variety, include slices of mushrooms, turnips, or crisp Chinese pea pods.

Cucumber Chile Dip. Peel 1 large **cucumber.** Cut in half lengthwise, and if seeds are large, scoop out with a spoon and discard. Cut cucumber in chunks. Using metal blade, process with on-off bursts until finely chopped; transfer to a bowl. Stir in ½ teaspoon **salt** and chill for at least 1 hour to release liquid.

Cut 1 small package (3 oz.) **cream cheese** in chunks and, using metal blade, process with 2 tablespoons **sour cream** until creamy. Cut 1 canned **green chile** (part of a 4-oz. can) in half, add to cheese mixture, and process with on-off bursts until chile is chopped. Drain liquid from cucumber; add cucumber to cheese mixture and process with 2 on-off bursts. Season to taste with **salt.** Makes 1 cup.

Creamy Spinach Dip. Cook 1 box (10 or 12 oz.) frozen chopped **spinach** according to package directions; drain, cool, and set aside. Cut 4 **green onions** and half of tops in 1-inch lengths. Using metal blade, process onions and ¾ cup packed **parsley** sprigs until finely chopped. Add 1 cup **mayonnaise,** 1 tablespoon **lemon juice,** ¼ teaspoon **salt,** ⅛ teaspoon ground **nutmeg,** and a dash **cayenne pepper;** process until blended.

Squeeze cooled spinach with your hands to press out all liquid; add spinach to mayonnaise mixture. Process with 2 on-off bursts or just enough to blend — spinach should not be puréed. Cover and chill before serving. Makes 2 cups.

Crunchy Egg Dip

(Pictured on page 47)

Offer this crunchy dip with an assortment of raw vegetables or spread on crisp shredded wheat crackers.

- 4 green onions
- ½ medium-size green pepper
- 1 small dill pickle
- 4 strips bacon, crisp-fried and drained
- 1 large package (8 oz.) Neufchâtel or cream cheese
- 1 tablespoon milk
- 4 hard-cooked eggs
  Salt and pepper

Cut onions and half of tops in 1-inch lengths. Using metal blade, process with on-off bursts until coarsely chopped. Seed green pepper; cut pepper and pickle in chunks and add to onions. Break bacon slices in half and add to onions. Process with on-off bursts until vegetables and bacon are coarsely chopped.

Cut cheese in chunks and add to bacon mixture along with milk. Process until cheese is softened. Shell eggs, cut in quarters, and distribute over cheese mixture. Process with 5 on-off bursts or until eggs are coarsely chopped. Season to taste with salt and pepper. Cover and chill. Makes about 3 cups.

Hot Crab Spread

For a party, serve this spread from a chafing dish fitted with a water jacket, or keep it hot in a double boiler and serve small batches from a pretty shell.

- 1 green onion
- 1 large package (8 oz.) cream cheese
- 1 tablespoon milk
- 1 teaspoon *each* Dijon mustard and prepared horseradish
- ½ teaspoon *each* Worcestershire and lemon juice
- 2 or 3 drops liquid hot pepper seasoning
- ½ cup cashews
- ½ pound (about 1⅓ cups) cooked fresh or canned crab

Cut onion and half of top in 1-inch lengths. Using metal blade, process onion until chopped. Cut cream cheese in chunks and, with motor running, drop pieces down feed tube; process with onion until smooth. Add milk, mustard, horseradish, Worcestershire, lemon juice, and hot pepper seasoning. Process for 2 seconds. Scrape side of bowl with a spatula, then process for 2 more seconds. Add nuts and process with 3 on-off bursts to coarsely chop nuts. Remove blade and stir in crab. (This much can be done ahead. Cover and chill.)

Before serving, heat mixture in a double boiler over hot water. Serve with an assortment of crackers and provide a knife for spreading. Makes 3 cups.

Avocado Tuna Spread

Here's a new twist to an old standby—tuna blended with avocado. Alfalfa sprouts are the option for those who like extra crunch.

- 3 green onions
- 1 medium-size green pepper
- ½ cup cottage cheese
- ½ teaspoon dry mustard
- 1½ teaspoons garlic salt
- 1 teaspoon prepared horseradish
- 1 large avocado
- 1 can (6½ oz.) tuna
  Crackers or whole wheat bread
  Alfalfa sprouts

Cut onions and tops in 1-inch lengths. Cut green pepper in chunks and discard seeds. Using metal blade, process onions and green pepper with on-off bursts until coarsely chopped. Add cottage cheese, mustard, garlic salt, and horseradish and process with 3 on-off bursts. Peel avocado, remove pit, and cut in chunks. Distribute avocado over cheese and process with on-off bursts until avocado is mashed. Drain tuna, break up with a fork, and distribute over cheese mixture. Process with 3 on-off bursts to blend. Makes 2½ cups spread.

For appetizers, serve tuna mixture in a bowl with crackers and alfalfa sprouts alongside. To eat, spread tuna on a cracker and top with sprouts. For sandwiches, toast and butter 10 thin slices whole wheat bread. Spread equal portions of tuna mixture over each of 5 slices, sprinkle each with about ¼ cup alfalfa sprouts, and top with remaining bread slices.

Spicy Clam Spread

Simple, well-seasoned spreads are always welcome. Serve on Melba toast for hot appetizers or on toasted English muffin halves for open-faced sandwiches.

- 1 green onion
- ½ cup cottage cheese
- ¼ teaspoon Worcestershire
- 1 tablespoon mayonnaise
- 1½ teaspoons lemon or lime juice
- ⅛ teaspoon *each* garlic salt and liquid hot pepper seasoning
- 1 can (8 oz.) minced clams
  Salt and pepper
- 16 pieces Melba toast or 2 English muffins, split, buttered, and toasted

Cut onion and top in 1-inch lengths. Using metal blade, process onion until chopped. Add cottage cheese, Worcestershire, mayonnaise, lemon juice, garlic salt, and hot pepper seasoning. Process for 3 seconds. Scrape sides of bowl with spatula and process for 3 more seconds. Drain clams (save liquid for soup), add to cheese, and process with 2 on-off bursts. Stir in salt and pepper to taste. (Cover and refrigerate if made ahead.)

Just before serving, spread mixture on Melba toast or English muffin halves. Place on a cooky sheet in a preheated broiler about 3 inches from heat. Broil until mixture is bubbly and heated through (about 3 minutes). Makes 16 appetizers or 4 open-faced sandwiches.

Spicy Ham Spread. Substitute 1 cup cooked **ham** cut in 1-inch cubes, for clams. First process ham with on-off bursts until finely chopped; set aside. Then prepare spread as directed but eliminate clams. When cheese mixture is smooth, add chopped ham and process for 2 seconds.

Tamalitos

You open these tiny, foil-wrapped tamales and eat them with your fingers.

2¼ cups masa harina (dehydrated masa flour)
1½ teaspoons salt
1¼ cups regular-strength chicken broth
½ cup salad oil
2 cups cooked chicken or turkey, cut in 1½-inch chunks
1 medium-size onion
1 can (4 oz.) chopped ripe olives
½ cup green chile salsa

Using metal blade, process masa harina and ½ teaspoon of the salt for 2 seconds. With the motor running, pour chicken broth and oil through feed tube, and process to make a thick paste; set aside.

Still using metal blade, process chicken with on-off bursts until coarsely chopped; set aside. Cut onion in chunks, then process with on-off bursts until coarsely chopped. Add remaining 1 teaspoon salt, olives, salsa, and chopped chicken and mix with 2 on-off bursts.

Cut 30 pieces of foil, each 6 inches square. Place about 1½ tablespoons masa paste on center of each foil square and spread it in a 3-inch square. Place about 1½ tablespoons chicken filling on each masa

(Continued on next page)

(Continued on next page)

Making Butter from a Nut

It is fascinating to watch a food processor make peanut butter. You drop whole nuts in the bowl fitted with the metal blade and turn the motor on. For a few seconds you hear the nuts clattering against the sides and top of the processor bowl. The noise stops as the nuts become mealy. In a minute or two a mass of ground nuts works its way down the sides of the bowl and the color darkens slightly. Seconds later, a ball of creamy butter forms at the bottom. It invites tasting. The peanut butter is slightly warm and marvelously fresh — good to scoop up with your finger or spread on a piece of bread.

Obviously, making your own nut butter is easy and enjoyable, but there are other advantages, too. You can make a completely natural spread. You can add salt or leave it out. You can blend two different kinds of nuts for new taste discoveries.

The best nuts to use for butters are peanuts, almonds, filberts, and cashews. Because pistachios, macadamias, and pine nuts are more expensive, they are better left for other uses. The astringent flavor of English walnuts, black walnuts, and pecans is too pronounced to make good-tasting butter. Chestnuts are too starchy to produce a buttery texture.

How to skin. Though it is not necessary to remove the skin of the nuts (also called "blanching"), nut butters taste richer and have a smoother texture if you do. To skin peanuts, roll the nuts between the palms of your hands. To blanch almonds, cover with boiling water and let stand for 5 minutes; then drain, slip off skins, and let the nuts dry in a single layer on paper towels.

You can blanch filberts by covering them with hot water for 15 minutes or toasting them until the thin skin is brittle enough to rub off. Place nuts in a single layer in a shallow pan. Roast in a 275° oven for 20 to 30 minutes, shaking occasionally. When cool, rub nuts between the palms of your hands to remove skins.

How to toast. Most of the nuts we buy have already been roasted, but an extra toasting brings out the rich flavor. Arrange nuts in a shallow pan in a single layer and bake in a 350° oven, shaking occasionally, until nuts are a pale golden brown (5 to 10 minutes).

If you have *raw* peanuts (with or without skins) or *raw* cashews, these should have longer toasting—10 to 15 minutes for peanuts, 15 to 20 minutes for cashews.

How to process. Process at least ½ pound (1½ cups) of shelled nuts at a time. This amount makes 1 cup of nut butter.

Peanuts turn into butter without any attention (though you can't help watching). But with other nuts, you need to turn the processor off and scrape the sides and bottom of the bowl with a spatula several times during processing to make sure the mixture is evenly blended. For creamy nut butter, process all nuts until the mixture forms a ball. Continue to process until mixture becomes very smooth and creamy. If you like a crunchy nut butter, you can stop the processing just short of the creamy stage.

How to store. Keep nut butter in a covered jar in the refrigerator or store in the freezer. It will become rancid quickly if left at room temperature, since it has no preservatives. Also, the oil may separate, unlike homogenized peanut butter, so stir well before using.

You can vary any nut butter by combining it with an equal amount of butter or margarine and chilling it until firm; this makes an excellent spread for canapés.

square, positioning it down the center. Fold foil edges together so that masa edges meet, then seal all sides.

To cook tamales, arrange in upper part of a steamer. Cover tightly and steam over boiling water for about 45 minutes. Serve hot. Makes 2½ dozen tamales.

Shrimp Toast

In Chinese restaurants, shrimp toast is fried in deep fat. Our version bakes in the oven, providing an appetizer that does not require last minute attention.

> 2 green onions
> 1 clove garlic
> 1 thin slice fresh ginger root (optional)
> 1 egg white
> 1½ teaspoons *each* cornstarch and dry sherry
> 1¼ teaspoons salt
> ½ cup water chestnuts
> ½ pound medium-size raw shrimp, shelled and deveined
> 8 thin slices firm white bread
> ¼ cup soft butter or margarine

Cut onions and tops in 1-inch lengths. Using metal blade, process onions, garlic, and ginger root (if desired) until coarsely chopped. Add egg white, cornstarch, sherry, and salt, and process for 2 seconds. Add water chestnuts and process with on-off bursts until coarsely chopped. Add shrimp and process with on-off bursts until finely chopped.

Remove bread crusts and spread butter on both sides of each slice. Spread shrimp mixture on 1 side of each slice, then cut each slice of bread twice on the diagonal to make 4 triangles. Place on a baking sheet. (At this point you can cover with clear plastic wrap and chill as long as 8 hours.) To cook, bake, uncovered, in a 375° oven for 10 minutes or until bread is toasted. Makes 32 appetizers.

Parsley Shrimp Balls

Shrimp balls—made with Neufchâtel cheese, rolled in parsley, and adorned with tiny shrimp — are low-calorie hors d'oeuvres that are tempting to non-calorie counters, too.

> 1⅓ cups packed parsley sprigs
> 1 clove garlic
> ½ stalk celery
> 4 ounces Neufchâtel cheese
> ¼ teaspoon liquid hot pepper seasoning
> 1 teaspoon soy sauce
> 10 ounces small cooked shrimp or 2 cans (about 5 oz. *each*) shrimp, rinsed and patted dry

Using metal blade, process parsley until finely chopped; set aside. Rinse processor bowl and blade and reassemble. Process garlic until chopped. Cut celery in chunks, add to garlic, and process with on-off bursts until finely chopped. Cut cheese in chunks and add to celery, along with hot pepper seasoning and soy sauce. Process with 2 on-off bursts, scrape sides of bowl with a spatula, then process until cheese is soft.

Set aside 40 whole shrimp for garnish. Add remaining shrimp to cheese mixture and process with 2 on-off bursts. Scrape sides of bowl with a spatula and process with 1 or 2 additional on-off bursts until shrimp are coarsely chopped. Cover and chill for 1 hour.

Sprinkle chopped parsley on a piece of wax paper. For each appetizer, shape 1 teaspoon of cheese mixture into a ball, then roll in parsley to coat all sides. Spear reserved shrimp on wooden picks and stick one shrimp into each ball. Cover and chill until serving. Makes 3 dozen appetizers.

Florentine Pâté

The name Florentine usually indicates that spinach is an integral part of a dish. In this case, though, it describes an Italian-style liver pâté, savory with the addition of anchovies and capers. Serve it freshly made while still warm; or, if made ahead, serve cold, and spread it generously on sliced rolls or toast.

> 1 large onion
> 1 stalk celery
> 1 large carrot
> ½ cup olive oil or salad oil
> 1 pound chicken livers or calf liver
> ¼ cup butter or margarine
> 6 anchovy fillets
> 2 tablespoons capers
> Pepper
> Chopped parsley and whole capers for garnish

Cut onion, celery, and carrot in chunks. Using metal blade, process each vegetable separately until finely chopped — use on-off bursts to chop the onion and celery. As each vegetable is chopped, transfer to a wide frying pan. Pour in oil and, stirring occasionally, cook over medium heat for 15 minutes or until vegetables are soft.

Cut chicken livers in half or, if using calf liver, cut in chunks. Add liver to vegetables and continue cooking for 5 to 7 minutes or until livers are firm but slightly pink in the center (cut a gash to test).

Meanwhile, cut butter into chunks and cut anchovies in half. Using metal blade, process butter, anchovies, and capers to make a smooth paste. Add liver mixture and process for 3 to 4 seconds until pâté is well mixed but still slightly lumpy. Season to taste with pepper.

Serve pâté while it is still warm. If you intend to serve it cold, chill first, then stir to reblend. To serve, mound pâté in a small dish and garnish with parsley and whole capers. Makes 3 cups.

Mushroom Almond Pâté

Masquerading as liver pâté, this creamy spread is meatless. Almonds supply the sweet nutlike flavor.

    1   cup slivered almonds
    1   clove garlic
    1   small onion
    ¾   pound mushrooms
    ¼   cup butter or margarine
    ¾   teaspoon salt
    ½   teaspoon thyme leaves
    ⅛   teaspoon white pepper
    2   tablespoons salad oil

Toast almonds in a wide frying pan over medium-low heat, stirring frequently, until lightly browned; turn out of pan and cool.

Using metal blade, process garlic until chopped. Cut onion in chunks, add to garlic, and process with on-off bursts until onion is chopped; set aside. Break mushrooms in half if large, drop in processor bowl, and process with on-off bursts until coarsely chopped. Melt butter in frying pan over medium-high heat. Add garlic, onion, mushrooms, salt, thyme, and pepper. Cook, stirring occasionally, until most liquid has evaporated.

Process almonds until coarsely chopped. Remove 2 tablespoons nuts and set aside. Process remaining nuts to form a paste. Pour oil down feed tube and process until creamy. Add mushroom mixture and process until pâté is smooth. Add reserved nuts and blend with 2 on-off bursts. Cover and chill if made ahead. Makes 2 cups.

Chicken Liver Pâté

Ultrasmooth and quick to make, this silken-textured pâté can be served with crackers for an hors d'oeuvre or sliced and presented with toast as a first course.

    ¼   pound mushrooms
    4   green onions
    ½   cup packed parsley sprigs
    ½   teaspoon each thyme leaves and salt
    1½ cups (¾ lb.) butter or margarine
    1   pound chicken livers, halved
    2   tablespoons brandy or Madeira
    ½   cup dry red wine

Using metal blade, process mushrooms with on-off bursts until coarsely chopped; set aside. Cut white part of onions in 1-inch lengths and process with

parsley, thyme, and salt until parsley is finely chopped. Melt ½ cup of the butter in a wide frying pan. Add chicken livers, mushrooms, and onion mixture. Cook, stirring often, over medium heat for about 5 minutes or until livers are just firm but slightly pink in center (cut a gash to test).

In small pan, warm brandy and set aflame (not beneath an exhaust fan or flammable items). Pour into pan with liver; shake pan until flame dies. Add wine, heat to simmering, and remove pan from heat. Cut remaining 1 cup butter in chunks. Transfer liver mixture and liquid to processor bowl. Process to make a smooth purée. With motor still running, drop pieces of butter down feed tube and process until smooth.

Pour pâté into a 4 or 5-cup serving container or several smaller containers; cover and chill overnight or up to 1 week; freeze for longer storage. Makes 12 to 16 servings.

Beef Tartare

This is a restaurant specialty that is a snap to duplicate at home. It is not necessary to use a deluxe cut of meat, but it is important to trim all the fat.

    1   clove garlic
    ½   small onion
    ½   pound top round or sirloin steak
    1   egg yolk
    ½   teaspoon each salt and Dijon mustard
    1   teaspoon each Worcestershire and capers
    ¼   teaspoon tarragon
    ⅛   teaspoon pepper
        Chopped parsley for garnish

Using metal blade, process garlic until chopped. Cut onion in chunks, add to garlic, and process with on-off bursts until chopped. Cut meat in 1-inch cubes; discard all fat and sinews. Add meat to onion along with egg yolk, salt, mustard, Worcestershire, capers, tarragon, and pepper. Process with on-off bursts until meat is coarsely chopped.

Mound mixture lightly into a serving container and chill until ready to use. Sprinkle with chopped parsley before serving. Present with an assortment of crackers. Makes about 1 cup.

Country Terrine

A terrine—a savory meat loaf that the French serve cold — is a very versatile dish. Traditionally, it is thickly sliced and presented with crusty bread and sour pickles as a first course. You might also feature it at lunch, a light supper, or a picnic accompanied by a salad; or slice it thinly for superb open-faced sandwiches. Assemble the terrine at least a day before you plan to serve it; the flavor improves as the seasonings mingle.

(Continued on next page)

6 strips bacon
1½ pounds beef liver, sliced ½ inch thick
3 tablespoons butter or margarine
1½ pounds boneless pork butt
3 green onions
2 eggs
2 tablespoons *each* all-purpose flour and
    brandy
2 teaspoons salt
1 teaspoon thyme leaves
½ teaspoon *each* marjoram leaves and
    ground allspice
¼ teaspoon white pepper
2 whole bay leaves
6 whole black peppers

Place bacon in a pan, cover with water, and bring to a boil. Reduce heat and simmer for 20 minutes; drain (this minimizes bacon's smoked flavor).

Trim any membrane from liver; cut liver in 1½-inch pieces. Melt butter in a large frying pan on medium-high heat; add liver and cook for about 3 minutes or until liver is slightly firm but still pink inside (cut a gash to test).

Using metal blade, process liver and pan drippings with 4 on-off bursts, or until it becomes a rough paste; transfer to a mixing bowl. Cut pork in 1-inch cubes and process ½ at a time with 4 on-off bursts or until finely chopped; add to liver paste.

Cut white part of the onions in 1-inch lengths. Process onions, eggs, flour, brandy, salt, thyme, marjoram, allspice, and pepper until onion is finely chopped. Pour over meat mixture and stir to blend. Process blended meat mixture, ⅓ at a time, to mix well and form a semismooth paste.

Arrange 3 of the prepared bacon strips lengthwise in bottom of a 9 by 5-inch loaf pan or a 6-cup straight-sided baking dish. Spread ground meat mixture in pan evenly. Cover with remaining 3 strips bacon. Place bay leaves and whole black peppers on top. Cover tightly with foil and set pan in a larger pan containing at least 1 inch scalding water. Bake in a 350° oven for 1 hour and 45 minutes or until juices run clear (cut a gash to test).

Remove from oven, and from larger pan. Uncover and let cool slightly at room temperature. Remove water from larger pan, and set terrine in it to catch any juices that might overflow. Cover terrine with a piece of heavy cardboard sealed in foil and cut to fit top of the terrine. Place a weight, such as canned goods, on top of cardboard to press down surface of terrine. A clean brick wrapped in foil is a convenient weight to fit in a loaf pan. (This step compacts meat as it cools.)

Chill terrine thoroughly. Use within a week; for longer storage, wrap airtight and freeze. To serve, immerse terrine in very hot water up to pan's rim, just until a little exterior fat begins to melt (takes only a few seconds). Turn meat onto a serving board, remove peppers and bay leaves, and scrape off fat. Cut into slices to serve. Makes 10 to 12 servings.

Terrine of Pork, Veal, and Ham

(Pictured on page 18)

Strips of ham and veal layered in the meat mixture create a decorative pattern when this terrine is sliced. For the pork back fat, ask at your meat market for a piece of fat cut from the loin.

6 strips bacon
1 veal cutlet (¼ lb.), cut ¼ inch thick
1 center-cut slice ham (¼ lb.), cut ¼ inch
    thick
1 small onion
3 tablespoons brandy
¼ teaspoon *each* ground allspice and thyme
    leaves
1 pound boneless veal stew
1 pound boneless pork butt
½ pound pork back fat
3 green onions
4 sprigs parsley
2 eggs
⅓ cup half-and-half (light cream)
2 teaspoons salt
1 teaspoon thyme leaves
½ teaspoon ground allspice
¼ teaspoon pepper
2 whole bay leaves
6 whole black peppers

Place bacon in a pan, cover with water, and bring to a boil. Reduce heat and simmer for 20 minutes; drain (this minimizes bacon's smoked flavor).

Cut veal cutlet and ham slice in strips ¼ inch wide. Using slicing disc, slice onion and add to meat strips along with brandy and the ¼ teaspoon *each* allspice and thyme. Let stand while you prepare ground meat mixture.

Cut veal, pork, and pork back fat in 1-inch cubes. Using metal blade, process 1 cup at a time until finely chopped. Transfer each batch to a large mixing bowl after it is chopped.

Cut white part only of green onions in 1-inch lengths and process with parsley until finely chopped. Drain brandy from marinated meat strips (discard sliced onion) and add to green onion-parsley mixture along with eggs, half-and-half, salt, the 1 teaspoon thyme, the ½ teaspoon allspice, and pepper. Process until blended. Pour over ground meat and stir. Process meat mixture, ⅓ at a time, to mix well — meat will be very finely ground, and pieces of pork fat will look about the size of a pin head.

Lay 3 strips prepared bacon in bottom of a 9 by 5-inch loaf pan. Spread ⅓ of ground meat mixture in pan; arrange ½ the ham and veal strips lengthwise in pan. Add another ⅓ of ground meat to pan, then top with remaining meat strips. Spread remaining ground meat on top and pat down. Cover with remaining 3 strips bacon. Place bay leaves and black peppers on top. Cover, bake, weight, and chill according to directions for country terrine (preceding recipe). Makes 10 to 12 servings.

Stuffed Mushrooms

Mushroom caps filled with a savory meat mixture and served hot make a delicious prelude to dinner. Arrange mushrooms on small plates and serve with forks.

     1 slice firm white bread
     4 green onions
    20 large or 40 medium-size mushrooms
     5 tablespoons butter or margarine
 1½ cups cooked ham, cut in 1-inch cubes
     1 package (9 oz.) frozen artichoke hearts, thawed
     1 egg
  ¼ teaspoon salt
     1 teaspoon marjoram leaves
     3 tablespoons grated Parmesan cheese
  ¼ cup dry white wine
       Parsley sprigs for garnish

Insert metal blade in food processor. Tear bread in chunks, then process to make fine, soft bread crumbs; set aside. Cut onions and half of tops in 1-inch lengths. Process with on-off bursts until coarsely chopped. Rinse mushrooms and remove stems; add stems to chopped onion and process until finely chopped. Turn mixture into a frying pan with 2 tablespoons of the butter and cook over medium heat until onion is limp.

Meanwhile, process ham until finely chopped; set aside. Process artichoke hearts with on-off bursts until coarsely chopped. Return ham to processor bowl along with bread crumbs, egg, salt, marjoram, and onion mixture; mix with 2 on-off bursts.

Melt remaining 3 tablespoons butter in a 9 by 13-inch baking pan. Turn mushroom caps in butter to coat. Heap equal amounts of filling in each mushroom cap and press it in firmly. Place mushrooms, filled side up, in pan and sprinkle with Parmesan cheese. Pour wine into pan. Bake in a 400° oven for 15 minutes. Serve hot, garnished with parsley. Makes about 8 to 10 servings.

Salami Turnovers

Wrapping a savory filling in tiny pastry rounds is time consuming, but the job is shortened considerably when you make the filling and the pastry in a food processor. These turnovers freeze well and can be popped in the oven at party time.

(Continued on page 19)

Seasoning with Herb Butters

(Fines Herbes Butter pictured on page 47)

If you like to get a head start on cooking, flavored butters will appeal to you. They are a quick way to season canapés or sandwiches before adding a topping or filling. And when you have a meal to prepare quickly, you can add a distinctive touch by melting some flavored butter on broiled steak, fish fillets, hamburger patties, poached eggs, or vegetables.

Because a food processor softens butter, you can start with butter right from the refrigerator and blend it with herbs and seasonings in seconds. If the mixture sticks to the sides of the processor bowl, scrape it down with a spatula and process for another second.

Store the flavored butter tightly covered in the refrigerator for as long as 2 weeks, or shape it into a log, wrap in foil, and freeze. Each recipe makes ½ cup.

Garlic Butter. Using metal blade, process 2 to 3 cloves **garlic** and ¼ cup packed **parsley** sprigs until finely chopped. Add ½ cup **butter** or margarine cut in chunks and process until well blended.

Melt on broiled salmon, lamb chops, or beef steaks. Heat on French bread or use to season boiled new potatoes.

Mustard Butter. Using metal blade, process ⅓ cup packed **parsley** sprigs until finely chopped. Add ½ cup **butter** or margarine cut in chunks, 2 teaspoons **dry mustard**, ½ teaspoon **Worcestershire**, ¼ teaspoon **garlic salt,** and a dash of **pepper;** process until well blended.

Spread on bread for meat or cheese sandwiches; use to season asparagus, zucchini, or carrots; melt on steak, hamburgers, sautéed liver, or fish.

Fines Herbes Butter. Cut only the white part of 1 **green onion** in 1-inch lengths. Using metal blade, process onion and ¼ cup packed **parsley** sprigs until finely chopped. Add ½ teaspoon *each* **tarragon** and **chervil**, ¼ teaspoon **salt,** dash of **pepper,** and ½ cup **butter** or margarine cut in chunks. Process until well blended.

Spread on appetizer sandwiches or French bread; melt on fillet of sole, poached eggs, sautéed liver, or corn on the cob.

4 ounces jack cheese
¼ pound dry salami, cut in 1-inch cubes
   (about 1½ cups)
1 can (6 oz.) tomato paste
½ teaspoon oregano leaves
¼ teaspoon garlic powder
   Pastry for 4 single-crust 9-inch pies or rich
   pie pastry (page 67)

Shred cheese with shredding disc and set aside. Change to metal blade. Process salami with on-off bursts until finely chopped. Add tomato paste, oregano, garlic powder, and cheese, and process with 4 on-off bursts or until filling is mixed.

On a lightly floured board, roll out about ¼ prepared pastry at a time, until ⅛ inch thick; cut into 2½ to 3-inch rounds. Place about ¾ teaspoon filling off-center on each round.

Dampen edges with water, fold pastry in half, press edges together with a fork, and prick tops. Place turnovers 2 inches apart on ungreased baking sheets and bake, uncovered, in a 450° oven for 10 minutes or until golden brown. Serve hot.

Or cool on wire racks, cover, and refrigerate until next day; for longer storage, wrap airtight and freeze. To reheat, bake, uncovered, in a 450° oven for 5 minutes (10 minutes if frozen) or until hot throughout. Makes 6 to 7 dozen turnovers.

Speedy Tortilla Pizza

A super-easy way to make appetizer pizza is to use Mexican flour tortillas. Provide plenty of napkins — this is messy to eat.

1 pound lean ground beef
¼ pound mushrooms
½ teaspoon salt
1 clove garlic, minced or pressed
1 can (7 oz.) green chile salsa
8 ounces jack or mozzarella cheese
1 small onion
½ green pepper
4 flour tortillas (about 8-inch size)
   Olive oil or salad oil
1 can (2¼ oz.) sliced ripe olives, drained
½ cup grated Parmesan cheese
1 avocado
1 cup sour cream

Crumble beef into a wide frying pan and cook, stirring, over medium heat until lightly browned and

ELABORATE HORS D'OEUVRES made simple with food processor magic. Clockwise, from upper left: Terrine of Pork, Veal, and Ham (page 16), Freezer Cheese Ball (page 10), prawns with Creamy Spinach Dip (page 11), Fila Cheese Onion Rolls (page 10).

crumbly (about 5 minutes); drain any excess fat. Meanwhile, insert slicing disc in food processor. Slice mushrooms and add to meat along with salt, garlic, and salsa. Cook, stirring, over high heat, until liquid has evaporated (about 3 to 5 minutes); remove from heat.

Change to shredding disc and shred jack cheese; set aside. Change to metal blade. Cut onion in chunks; cut green pepper in chunks and discard seeds. Process onion and green pepper separately with on-off bursts until coarsely chopped.

Brush tortillas lightly with oil on both sides, being sure edges are oiled. Place tortillas slightly apart on shallow baking pans. Spread meat sauce evenly over tortillas; then scatter onion, green pepper, and sliced olives evenly over sauce. Sprinkle jack cheese in an even layer over vegetables; then sprinkle with Parmesan cheese.

Bake in a 475° oven until cheese melts and is lightly browned (about 7 to 10 minutes). Peel avocado, remove pit, and dice with a knife; sprinkle over tops of pizzas. Cut each pizza in 6 wedges. Pass sour cream to spoon over servings. Makes 4 dozen appetizers.

Salsa Meatballs

Serving bite-size meatballs in a chafing dish leaves you free to enjoy your party while guests help themselves.

2 slices bread, dried until crisp
2 cloves garlic
¼ cup packed parsley sprigs
1 small onion
1 egg
¼ cup milk
½ teaspoon salt
1 pound lean ground beef
1 can (10½ oz.) condensed consommé
1 can (7 oz.) green chile salsa
3 tablespoons catsup
¼ teaspoon liquid hot pepper seasoning

Break bread in pieces and drop into food processor bowl fitted with metal blade. Process to make ½ cup fine crumbs; set aside. Process garlic and parsley until finely chopped. Cut onion in chunks, add to parsley, and process with on-off bursts until onion is chopped medium-fine. Add egg, milk, salt, and reserved bread crumbs. Process with 2 on-off bursts. Add meat and process just until mixture is blended. Shape into balls the size of large marbles.

Arrange meatballs on shallow baking pans. Bake in a 500° oven for 8 to 10 minutes or until browned.

In a large frying pan, over low heat, combine consommé, salsa, catsup, and hot pepper seasoning. Simmer for 10 to 12 minutes or until sauce is thickened. Drain meatballs and combine with sauce before serving. Makes about 5 dozen appetizers.

Soups & Salads

Making soups and salads is an effortless way to prepare good food while you get acquainted with your food processor. Slice, chop, and mince vegetables for main-dish soups. For satin-smooth soups, go one step further and purée the vegetables once they are cooked. When puréeing, keep in mind the capacity of the food processor bowl— you'll certainly want to avoid overflows.

For green salads, tear the lettuce by hand. But from that point on, leave the work for the food processor—it does everything from preparing the other vegetables and garnishes to blending the salad dressing.

French Onion Soup

Cooking the onions very slowly until they take on a rich caramel color is the secret of making good onion soup. For a lighter dish, eliminate the crusty cheese topping and simply garnish the soup with grated Parmesan cheese.

- 6 large onions
- 1 tablespoon olive oil or salad oil
- 2 tablespoons butter or margarine
- 1 tablespoon all-purpose flour
- 6 cups regular-strength beef broth
  Salt and pepper
- ⅓ cup dry red wine
- 4 ounces Swiss cheese
- 6 slices French bread (each ½ inch thick), toasted and buttered

Insert slicing disc in food processor. Cut onions in half lengthwise so they will stand in feed tube and slice. Put olive oil and butter in a 3 to 4-quart pan. Add onion slices and cook slowly, uncovered, over medium-low heat until onion is limp and caramel-colored, but not browned (about 40 minutes). Stir in flour and cook slowly, stirring continually until flour is slightly browned (about 2 minutes). Pour about 1 cup of the broth into onion-flour mixture, stirring to blend flour and broth. Add remaining broth and bring to a boil, stirring. Reduce heat, cover, and simmer for 30 minutes. Sprinkle with salt and pepper to taste and stir in wine. (This much can be done ahead. Cover and chill; then reheat to continue.)

Change to shredding disc and shred cheese. Ladle hot soup into 6 individual ovenproof soup bowls. Set a piece of toasted French bread on top of soup in each bowl and sprinkle equally with shredded cheese. Place bowls in a 425° oven for 10 minutes; then broil about 4 inches from heat until cheese browns. Makes 6 main-dish servings.

Curried Split Pea Soup

Serve this main-dish soup with hot, crusty bread for a family lunch or supper.

- 1 medium-size onion
- 4 strips bacon
- 1 clove garlic
- 1 cup dried yellow split peas
- 5 cups water
- 1 large carrot
- 2 stalks celery
- 1 can (about 1 lb.) tomatoes
- 1 teaspoon each salt and curry powder
- ¼ teaspoon pepper
- ¼ cup packed parsley sprigs

Cut onion in chunks. Cut bacon crosswise in 4 sections. (Use bacon directly from refrigerator so it is still firm.) Using metal blade, process onion, bacon, and garlic with on-off bursts until coarsely chopped. Turn into a 3-quart saucepan along with peas and water. Cover and simmer until peas are tender (about 1 hour).

Still using metal blade, process soup, ½ at a time, until smooth. Return purée to pan. Cut carrot and celery into chunks. Process separately until coarsely chopped, using on-off bursts for celery;

add to soup. Process tomatoes and their liquid with 3 on-off bursts to break tomatoes into small chunks; pour into soup. Season with salt, curry powder, and pepper. Cover and simmer until vegetables are tender (about 25 minutes).

Process parsley until finely chopped. Stir into soup just before serving. Makes 6 main-dish servings.

Mushroom Velvet Soup

Because this soup takes only 10 minutes to prepare, it is an easy first course for a party. Offer cups of soup to your guests for sipping before they come to the table.

- ½ pound mushrooms
- 1 medium-size onion
- ⅔ cup packed parsley sprigs
- ¼ cup butter or margarine
- 1 tablespoon all-purpose flour
- 1 can (14 oz.) regular-strength beef broth
- 1 cup sour cream

Insert slicing disc in food processor. Slice mushrooms and set aside. Change to metal blade. Cut onion in chunks and process with on-off bursts until coarsely chopped; set aside. Process parsley until finely chopped. Melt butter in a wide frying pan over medium-high heat. Add mushrooms and chopped vegetables, and cook, stirring, until mushrooms are limp and all juices have evaporated (about 5 minutes). Stir in flour; remove from heat and blend in beef broth. Bring to a boil, stirring.

Using metal blade, process ½ of the soup with ½ of the sour cream until smooth. Repeat for other ½ of the soup and sour cream. (This much can be done ahead. Cover and refrigerate until next day; reheat to serve.) Makes 6 first-course servings.

Cream of Cauliflower Soup

(Pictured on page 34)

Carrots and cauliflower supply the garden-fresh taste to this soup. Serve it as a first course or for lunch or supper with turkey or ham sandwiches.

- 1 large onion
- 2 tablespoons butter or margarine
- 2 cans (about 14 oz. each) regular-strength chicken broth
- 2 medium-size carrots
- 1 medium-size cauliflower
- 1 cup half-and-half (light cream)
- ⅛ teaspoon ground nutmeg
  Salt and pepper
- 1 tablespoon dry sherry (optional)
- ¼ cup packed parsley sprigs

Insert slicing disc in food processor. Cut onion in pieces to fit feed tube and slice. Place onion slices and butter in a 3-quart pan and cook over medium heat until onion is limp (about 5 minutes). Pour in chicken broth and bring to a boil.

Meanwhile, cut carrots in lengths to fit feed tube; slice. Trim leaves from cauliflower and cut in pieces to fit feed tube; slice. Add carrots and cauliflower to boiling broth, reduce heat, and simmer, covered, until vegetables are tender (about 15 minutes).

Change to metal blade and process soup, ½ at a time, until smooth. Return puréed soup to 3-quart pan; add half-and-half, nutmeg, salt and pepper to taste, and sherry; heat to simmering.

Rinse processor bowl and blade and reassemble. Process parsley until finely chopped. Sprinkle parsley over soup before serving. Makes 6 first-course servings.

North Beach Minestrone

(Pictured on page 23)

Don't overlook this recipe because the ingredient list is long. You prepare most of the elements in the food processor. The quantity will provide enough for a soup party plus extra to freeze.

- 1 pound dried cranberry beans or pink beans
- 4 quarts water
- 4 marrow beef bones, each 3 inches long
- 4 slices meaty beef shanks, each 1 inch thick
- 2 large onions
- 6 tablespoons olive oil or salad oil
- 2 large carrots
- 2 stalks celery
- 1 bunch leeks
- 1 can (about 1 lb.) tomatoes
  About 3 teaspoons salt
- ½ pound green beans
- 2 or 3 large potatoes
- 1 cup packed parsley sprigs
- 1 clove garlic
- ¼ cup fresh basil leaves or 2 tablespoons dry basil
- ½ small head cabbage
- 4 small zucchini
- ½ cup salad macaroni
  Grated Parmesan cheese

In a 10-quart kettle, combine beans and water, bring to boiling, and boil for 2 minutes; remove from heat and let stand, covered, for 1 hour. Then add marrow bones and beef shanks; bring to boiling, reduce heat, and simmer for 2 hours. Remove meat and bones from stock and cool slightly. Pull lean meat from bones and shred; scoop marrow from bones. Reserve meat and marrow and discard bones.

With a slotted spoon, remove half of beans from

stock and place in food processor bowl fitted with metal blade. Process until smooth. Return puréed beans to stock along with reserved meat.

Cut onions in chunks and, using metal blade, process with on-off bursts until coarsely chopped. Heat 4 tablespoons of the oil in a wide frying pan, add onions, and cook over medium-high heat until soft. Cut carrots and celery into chunks. Split leeks in half lengthwise, wash thoroughly, then cut in 1-inch lengths; discard tough green tops. Process carrots, celery, and leeks separately until coarsely chopped — use on-off bursts to chop celery and leeks. Add chopped vegetables to onion and cook together for 5 minutes over medium heat. Process tomatoes and their liquid with 3 on-off bursts to break tomatoes into chunks; add to onion mixture and simmer rapidly for 10 minutes or until most of liquid has evaporated. Add onion mixture to beans and simmer for 30 minutes. Season with salt.

Meanwhile, with a knife, cut green beans into 2-inch pieces; set aside. Peel potatoes, cut into chunks, and process, 1 at a time, with on-off bursts until coarsely chopped; set aside. Process parsley, garlic, and basil until finely chopped; set aside. Change to slicing disc. Cut cabbage in wedges and zucchini in lengths to fit feed tube; slice and set aside.

Stir green beans and potatoes into soup. Simmer rapidly, uncovered, for 10 minutes; then add cabbage, zucchini, and macaroni. Simmer for 5 additional minutes.

In another pan, over medium heat, cook chopped parsley mixture in remaining 2 tablespoons oil until parsley is bright green. Mix into soup just before serving. Taste and add salt if desired. Pass Parmesan cheese to sprinkle over each serving. Makes 12 to 14 main-dish servings.

Vichyssoise

Potato lends thickness and body to this delicately flavored leek soup. Vichyssoise is traditionally served cold, but the flavors take well to hot presentation, too.

    4 leeks or 1 large bunch green onions
    1 large onion
    ¼ cup butter or margarine
    3 large potatoes
    4 cups regular-strength chicken broth
    ½ pint whipping cream
       About 1 cup milk
    1 teaspoon salt
    ¼ teaspoon white pepper
       Chopped chives or green onion tops for
          garnish

Split leeks in half lengthwise so you can wash thoroughly, then cut in 1-inch lengths; discard tough green tops. Or cut white part of green onions in

1-inch lengths. Using metal blade, process leeks or green onions with on-off bursts until coarsely chopped. Place in a 3-quart kettle.

Cut onion in chunks and process with on-off bursts until coarsely chopped. Add to leeks along with butter and cook over low heat until onion is soft but not browned.

Peel potatoes, cut in chunks, and process, 1 at a time, with on-off bursts until coarsely chopped. Add to onion mixture along with chicken broth. Bring to a boil; then reduce heat, cover and simmer until potatoes are tender (about 20 minutes).

Still using metal blade, process ½ of the soup at a time until smooth. Pour puréed soup into a bowl, stir in cream and milk, then season with salt and pepper. If too thick, thin with additional milk. Chill thoroughly. Serve cold, sprinkled with chives or green onion tops. Makes 6 first-course servings.

Icy Gazpacho

The variations of this Spanish specialty are many. This one is best described as a cooling salad in soup form. It makes a refreshing opener for hot-weather meals.

    1 cucumber
    ½ green pepper, seeded
    1 small onion
    2 tomatoes
    ½ avocado
    4 cups tomato juice
    3 tablespoons olive oil or salad oil
    2 tablespoons wine vinegar
    ½ teaspoon crumbled oregano leaves
       Salt
       Ice cubes

Peel cucumber and cut in half lengthwise. If seeds are large, scoop out with a spoon and discard, then cut cucumber in chunks. Using metal blade, process cucumber with on-off bursts until coarsely chopped; transfer to a mixing bowl. Cut green pepper and onion in chunks. Process separately with on-off bursts until finely chopped; add to cucumber.

Peel tomatoes and, with a knife, cut in ¼-inch cubes. Peel avocado and cut in ½-inch cubes with a knife. Add tomatoes and avocado to cucumber along with tomato juice, olive oil, vinegar, oregano, and salt to taste. Chill for at least 2 hours or until next day. To serve, ladle into bowls and add 2 ice cubes to each bowl. Makes 8 first-course servings.

HEARTY, SAVORY North Beach Minestrone (page 21) combines many herbs and vegetables with high-protein pinto beans and meat.

Salad Dressings in Seconds

The terrific advantage of preparing salad dressing in a food processor is that flavoring ingredients can be added whole. Herbs and seasonings are chopped almost instantly, and recipes that call for blending or emulsifying are made in a flash.

All of the following dressings can be prepared for immediate serving. Chilling them for several hours helps to blend the flavors, though, and they will keep for as long as a week in the refrigerator.

Blue Cheese Dressing

Increase the buttermilk in this recipe if you prefer a thinner dressing.

- 1 cup mayonnaise
- 2 ounces (¼ cup) blue cheese
- ½ cup sour cream
- 1 tablespoon grated Parmesan cheese
- 2 tablespoons buttermilk
  Dash of garlic powder

Using metal or plastic blade, process mayonnaise, blue cheese, sour cream, Parmesan cheese, buttermilk, and garlic powder for 4 seconds or until well blended. Dressing should still show small lumps of blue cheese. Makes 1¼ cups.

Tomato French Dressing

Serve this sweet, tangy dressing on a tossed green salad or over cold cooked vegetables.

- ¼ small onion
- 1 small clove garlic
- ½ cup *each* salad oil and vinegar
- ½ can (10¾ oz.) condensed tomato soup
- 1 teaspoon Worcestershire
- 1 tablespoon sugar
- ½ teaspoon *each* salt, paprika, and dry mustard

Using metal blade, process onion and garlic with on-off bursts until finely chopped. Add oil, vinegar, soup, Worcestershire, sugar, salt, paprika, and mustard; process for 5 seconds to blend. Makes 1½ cups.

Green Goddess Dressing

For a traditional presentation, mix this dressing with crisp greens, spoon onto individual salad plates, and garnish with cooked shrimp, crab meat, or chicken.

- 3 anchovy fillets
- 3 green onions
- 1 small clove garlic
- ½ cup packed parsley sprigs
- ½ teaspoon tarragon
- 2 tablespoons tarragon vinegar
- 1½ cups mayonnaise (can use part sour cream)

Cut anchovy fillets in half. Cut green onions and half of tops in 1-inch lengths. Using metal blade, process anchovies, onions, garlic, and parsley until finely chopped. Add tarragon, vinegar, and mayonnaise; process for 5 seconds to blend. Makes 1½ cups.

Mayonnaise

The secret of making mayonnaise is to add the oil as slowly as possible. Measure the oil into a cup with a lip so you can rest the lip of the cup on top of the feed tube while you pour in the oil. This will make it easier to pour very slowly.

Whole egg mayonnaise is softer than mayonnaise made with egg yolks alone. But egg yolks not only make a thicker, stiffer sauce, they also add a richer flavor. Your taste determines your choice.

- 1 whole large egg or 3 egg yolks
- 1 teaspoon Dijon (or other style) mustard
- 1 tablespoon wine vinegar or lemon juice
- 1 cup salad oil
  Salt and pepper

Using metal or plastic blade, process egg, mustard, and vinegar for 3 seconds to blend well. With processor still running, add oil, a few drops at a time at first, then increasing to a slow, steady stream about $1/16$ inch wide. As you add oil, mayonnaise will thicken. Taste and season with a few more drops of vinegar and salt and pepper, if desired. Makes 1 cup.

Chutney Mayonnaise. Prepare mayonnaise as directed but use metal blade. Add 2 to 4 tablespoons **chutney** and process until it is finely chopped. Serve on fruit salad.

Green Mayonnaise. Prepare mayonnaise as directed, but use metal blade. Place 8 sprigs **watercress,** 6 **spinach** leaves, and 5 sprigs **parsley** in a bowl and cover with boiling water. Let stand 6 minutes; drain and rinse in cold water, then drain again. Place in processor with prepared mayonnaise. Add 2 teaspoons **lemon juice.** Process until blended. Serve with seafood salad.

Overnight Layered Green Salad

(Pictured on page 28)

Here is a handsome and colorful salad, perfect for holiday parties or a summer buffet. Assembly is simple—each layer goes directly from the food processor to the serving container.

- 1 medium-size head iceberg lettuce, washed and chilled
- 1 bunch green onions
- 1 can (8 oz.) water chestnuts
- ½ red bell or green pepper, seeded
- 2 stalks celery
- 1 package (10 oz.) frozen peas
- 2 cups mayonnaise
- 2 teaspoons sugar
- ½ cup grated Parmesan cheese
- 1 teaspoon salt
- ¼ teaspoon garlic powder
- ¾ pound bacon, crisp-fried and drained
- 3 hard-cooked eggs
- 2 tomatoes

Insert slicing disc in food processor. Core lettuce and cut in wedges that will stand in feed tube; slice. Spread lettuce over bottom of a wide 4-quart serving dish. With a knife, thinly slice green onions and part of the tops (because of their texture and shape, green onions cannot be sliced neatly in the food processor). Scatter slices over lettuce.

Drain water chestnuts, drop into feed tube, and slice; sprinkle over onions. Stand red pepper vertically in feed tube and slice; sprinkle over water chestnuts. Cut celery in lengths to fit feed tube and slice; sprinkle over red pepper.

Open package of frozen peas and break apart. Sprinkle frozen peas over salad. Spread mayonnaise evenly over peas. Sprinkle with sugar, Parmesan cheese, salt, and garlic powder.

Change to metal blade and process bacon until finely chopped; sprinkle over salad. Wash bowl and blade and reassemble. Cut eggs in quarters, drop into processor bowl, and process with on-off bursts until coarsely chopped. Sprinkle over bacon. Cover and chill for 4 hours or as long as 24 hours.

Just before serving, cut tomatoes in wedges and arrange around top of salad. To serve, use a spoon and fork to lift out each serving, which should include some of each layer. Makes 8 to 10 servings.

Mushroom Salad

If you've always sliced mushrooms by hand, you'll welcome the fast and thin slicing your processor will do. And if the only raw mushrooms you've eaten have been marinated, be prepared for a complete flavor change. This salad is light and mild—a good starting point for a meal featuring a highly seasoned entrée. The bit of mayonnaise, an unusual ingredient in this type of dressing, supplies body and flavor.

- ½ pound medium-size mushrooms
- ½ cup packed parsley sprigs
- 1 small clove garlic
- ⅓ cup salad oil
- 2 tablespoons white wine vinegar
- 1 tablespoon mayonnaise
- ½ teaspoon salt
- ⅛ teaspoon *each* dry mustard and pepper
- 6 to 9 butter lettuce leaves, washed and chilled

Wash and drain mushrooms; trim base of each stem. Slice mushrooms with slicing disc; transfer slices to a bowl. Change to metal blade. Process parsley until finely chopped; combine with mushrooms. Cover and chill until ready to serve.

Cut garlic in half and, still using metal blade, process until finely chopped. Add oil, vinegar, mayonnaise, salt, mustard, and pepper and process for 5 seconds to blend. Just before serving, pour dressing over mushrooms and toss until well mixed. Arrange 2 or 3 butter lettuce leaves on each individual serving plate and spoon salad onto center of leaves. Makes 2 to 3 servings.

California Coleslaw

If you like coarsely shredded cabbage for your slaw, use the slicing disc. For smaller, more uniform pieces, use the shredding disc.

- 1 small head (about 1½ lbs.) cabbage
- 2 stalks celery
- 1 small cucumber
- ½ green pepper
- 2 green onions
- ¼ cup packed parsley sprigs
- 6 strips bacon, crisp-fried and drained
- ¼ cup *each* mayonnaise and sour cream
- 1 tablespoon lemon juice
- ½ teaspoon *each* salt and sugar
  Dash *each* pepper and paprika

Cut cabbage in wedges to fit feed tube. Using slicing or shredding disc, process cabbage; transfer to a bowl. Cut celery in lengths to fit feed tube, process with slicing disc, then add to cabbage.

Change to metal blade. Peel cucumber and cut in chunks. Remove seeds from green pepper and cut in chunks. Process cucumber and green pepper separately using on-off bursts until coarsely chopped. Add to cabbage. Cut green onions and part of the tops in 1-inch lengths; process with parsley until finely chopped, then add to cabbage. Process bacon until finely chopped; add to cabbage.

(Continued on page 27)

. . . California Coleslaw (cont'd.)

Use metal or plastic blade to make dressing. Process together mayonnaise, sour cream, lemon juice, salt, sugar, pepper, and paprika. Pour over cabbage mixture and toss lightly. Makes 6 to 8 servings.

Caesar Salad from the Kitchen

When you are hungry for the robust flavor of a Caesar salad but don't want to stage a dramatic assembly at the table, try this recipe. The dressing can be made ahead but should not be stored longer than 2 days.

    2   tablespoons butter or margarine
    2   slices bread, cut into ½-inch cubes
    2   cloves garlic
    6   to 8 anchovy fillets
    ¼   cup olive oil or salad oil
    2   tablespoons grated Parmesan cheese
    2   tablespoons lemon juice
    1   egg yolk (raw)
    1½ teaspoons Worcestershire
    ⅛   teaspoon freshly ground pepper
    1   large head romaine lettuce, washed and
          chilled

Melt butter in a frying pan; add bread cubes and 1 whole clove garlic. Stirring occasionally, cook over medium heat until croutons are toasted; discard garlic.

Cut remaining clove of garlic in half. Using metal blade, process garlic until finely chopped. Cut anchovies in half. Add to garlic along with oil, Parmesan cheese, lemon juice, egg yolk, Worcestershire, and pepper. Process until anchovies are finely chopped.

Just before serving, tear romaine into bite-size pieces and place in a salad bowl. Pour dressing over lettuce and toss until every leaf is glossy. Add croutons, mix gently, and serve immediately. Makes 4 to 6 servings.

Zucchini Salad

Unlike marinated cucumbers, which become slightly limp, zucchini retains its crispness even when served the next day. The flavor of the dressing is similar to that used on light Japanese salads.

CRISP AND COOL Overnight Layered Green Salad (page 25) makes a refreshing summer lunch with Petites Brioches (page 71).

    4   medium-size zucchini
    2   green onions
    1   small green pepper, seeded
    1   stalk celery
    ¼   cup each sugar and white vinegar
    3   tablespoons salad oil
    ½   teaspoon salt
        Dash of monosodium glutamate

Cut zucchini in lengths to stand in feed tube and process with slicing disc; transfer zucchini slices to a bowl. Change to metal blade. Cut green onions and tops in 1-inch lengths and process with on-off bursts until coarsely chopped. Cut green pepper and celery in chunks, add to onion, and process with on-off bursts until finely chopped. Add chopped vegetables to zucchini. Process together sugar, vinegar, oil, salt, and monosodium glutamate until well blended. Pour over zucchini and mix. Cover and chill for 1 hour or as long as 2 days. Makes 6 to 8 servings.

Tabbuli

An adaptation of a classic Middle Eastern dish, this clean-tasting salad features cracked wheat and finely chopped vegetables. You can eat it with a fork, but it tastes even better when you scoop up each bite with a piece of romaine. As a variation, you can spoon this into hollowed-out tomatoes.

    1   cup bulgur wheat
    1   cup water
    ⅓   cup olive oil or salad oil
    ¼   cup lemon juice
    1½ teaspoons salt
    1   teaspoon ground allspice
    1   bunch green onions
    ⅓   cup lightly packed fresh mint leaves
    1½ cups packed parsley sprigs
    2   tomatoes
    1   head romaine lettuce, washed and chilled

Bring bulgur and water to a boil in a covered pan. Immediately reduce heat and simmer for 5 minutes or until liquid is absorbed; bulgur should still be crunchy. Turn bulgur into a bowl and mix with oil, lemon juice, salt, and allspice.

Cut green onions and tops in 1-inch lengths. Using metal blade, process onions and mint leaves until finely chopped; add to bulgur. Process parsley until finely chopped; add to bulgur. With a knife, cut tomatoes in ¼-inch cubes. Add to bulgur and mix all together lightly. Cover and chill for 1 hour or until next day.

To serve, line a platter or chop plate with large outside romaine leaves; pile tabbuli in center. Arrange remaining romaine leaves on a second plate. To eat tabbuli, tear off a piece of romaine and use it to scoop up each bite. Makes 6 to 8 servings.

Main Dish Meats

Rather than investigate all the short cuts you can take with a food processor just to prepare meats, this chapter presents a variety of processor techniques you can use to create truly delicious meat dishes. We also explore the ways that effort (notably reduced when you use a food processor), instead of expensive ingredients, can produce a memorable entrée. The range of recipes is international, but all will be at home on your own table.

Norwegian Meatballs

Adequate browning is the secret of the rich flavor and color of these meatballs. First you brown the meatballs well, then you slowly brown the flour in the pan drippings to make the gravy.

> 2 slices white bread
> ¾ cup milk
> 1 egg
> 1½ teaspoons salt
> ¼ teaspoon *each* pepper, ground allspice, and ground ginger
> ¼ pound ground pork
> 2 pounds lean ground beef
> 2 tablespoons butter or margarine
> 1 medium-size onion (optional)
> ¼ cup all-purpose flour, unsifted
> 2 cups water
> Salt and pepper

Fit metal blade in food processor bowl. Tear bread in pieces, drop in bowl, and process to make soft crumbs. Add milk, egg, salt, pepper, allspice, ginger, and pork. Process with 1 long burst or until well mixed. Distribute ½ of ground beef over pork mixture and process 5 seconds. Add remaining ground beef and process with 3 or 4 long bursts or until well mixed. (This processing makes a fine-grained, tender meatball usually achieved by vigorous kneading.) With wet hands (to prevent meat from sticking), roll meat mixture into walnut-size balls, or even smaller if you wish.

Melt butter in a wide frying pan over medium-high heat. Add meatballs, a portion at a time, and brown them on all sides. Using a slotted spoon, transfer meatballs, as browned, to a 2-quart casserole. Pour off all but 1 tablespoon pan drippings; reserve remaining drippings.

If using onion, change to slicing disc and slice.

Then add onion to the 1 tablespoon pan drippings and, stirring occasionally, cook over medium-high heat until soft but not browned (about 2 minutes). Spoon onion over meatballs.

Return 2 tablespoons of the reserved drippings to pan, add flour, and cook, stirring, over low heat until flour has turned golden brown. Gradually pour in water and cook, stirring, until gravy is smooth and thickened. Season to taste with salt and pepper. Pour gravy over meatballs. (At this point you can cover and refrigerate as long as overnight.)

To serve, bake, covered, in a 350° oven for 45 minutes (55 minutes if refrigerated). Makes 6 to 8 servings.

Beef and Vegetable Sauté

Steamed rice is all you need to complete a meal when you serve this colorful dish, quickly cooked and seasoned with a light sweet-sour sauce.

> 2 large carrots
> 2 medium-size zucchini
> 1 large onion
> ¼ pound fresh green beans
> 1 to 1¼ pounds top round or flank steak
> 3 tablespoons salad oil
> 1 cup water
> ⅓ cup firmly packed brown sugar
> 2 tablespoons cornstarch
> ¼ cup vinegar
> 3 tablespoons soy sauce

Using slicing disc, slice carrots and set aside. Slice zucchini and onion. With a knife, cut green beans into 1-inch lengths.

Cut meat in half lengthwise; slice each half crosswise on the diagonal into ⅛-inch-thick strips. Heat 2 tablespoons of the oil in a wide frying pan over high heat; add meat, ½ at a time, and cook, stirring frequently, until slices are browned on the outside but still slightly pink in the middle (about 2 minutes). Set aside.

In same pan, heat remaining 1 tablespoon oil. Add carrots and beans and toss once. Add ½ cup of the water, cover, and cook over medium-high heat for 3 minutes. Add zucchini and onion, turn heat to high, and cook for 2 minutes longer or until vegetables are just tender-crisp. Combine sugar, cornstarch, vinegar, soy, and remaining ½ cup water. Stir into vegetables, return meat to pan, and cook, stirring, until sauce has thickened (about 30 seconds). Makes 4 to 6 servings.

Meat Loaf in a Bread Basket

(Pictured on page 34)

A festive meat loaf is this one that comes to the table —or to a picnic—encased in a crusty loaf of bread. But unless you grind the meat yourself (see page 36 for directions), you're likely to end up with bread that's soggy, not crusty; superlean meat is absolutely necessary. For bread, choose either the brown and serve type or fully baked, and make it sourdough if it's available where you live.

- 1 large round loaf unsliced French bread, about 9 inches in diameter (may use brown and serve bread or completely baked bread)
- ½ cup milk
- ½ cup packed parsley sprigs
- 1 small tomato
- 2 eggs
- 1½ teaspoons salt
- ⅛ teaspoon pepper
- ¼ teaspoon *each* oregano leaves and dry basil
- ½ pound *each* lean ground beef, ground pork, and ground veal
- 2 ounces jack cheese
- 2 tablespoons butter or margarine, at room temperature

Slice off a 7-inch circle from top of loaf to form lid. Pull enough soft bread out of loaf and from inside lid to leave a ½-inch-thick shell. Using metal blade, process enough of the soft bread to make 1 cup crumbs (save remaining bread for other uses).

Turn crumbs into a large mixing bowl, stir in milk, and let stand 5 minutes. Process parsley until finely chopped; add to bread crumbs. Peel tomato, cut into chunks, and process with on-off bursts until coarsely chopped. Add eggs, salt, pepper, oregano, and basil to tomato and process 2 seconds

to blend. Add to bread crumbs along with ground meats and mix well. Pack meat mixture into bread shell.

Shred cheese with the shredding disc. Sprinkle over meat, then replace bread lid — it should fit tightly on bread. Rub butter on all sides of loaf. Wrap buttered loaf in a piece of heavy-duty foil or a double thickness of lightweight foil; place on a baking sheet.

Bake in a 350° oven for 2 hours. Remove from oven and loosen foil to allow steam to escape. (If you use brown and serve bread, open foil for the last 10 minutes of baking so bread can brown.) Cool for 10 minutes, then cut in wedges with a serrated knife.

If you wish to keep bread warm for several hours, loosen foil and allow steam to escape, then rewrap in foil. Makes 10 servings.

Beef Fillets in Flaky Pastry

When you plan a special occasion and time is short, try this elegant entrée. The flaky pastry wrapper is achieved quickly, thanks to frozen puff patty shells, and it can all be assembled a day ahead.

- 1 tablespoon butter or margarine
- 6 small beef fillet steaks (3 or 4 oz. *each*), cut 1 inch thick and trimmed of fat
- 6 tablespoons Madeira or dry sherry
- ½ cup duxelles (page 50)
- 6 frozen patty shells (one 10-oz. package), thawed
  Salt
  Béarnaise cream sauce (recipe follows)

Melt butter in a wide frying pan over highest heat and sear steaks on each side just to give brown color. Pour 2 tablespoons of the Madeira over meat, then transfer steaks to another container, cover, and chill thoroughly.

To frying pan add remaining 4 tablespoons Madeira. Crumble in duxelles and cook over medium-low heat, stirring, until all liquid has evaporated. Cover and chill duxelles mixture.

Roll out thawed pastries, 1 at a time, on a lightly floured board, to make circles about 8 inches in diameter (it doesn't matter which pastry side is up). Put ⅙ of duxelles mixture in center of each pastry, set 1 cold steak on top, sprinkle lightly with salt, fold all 4 pastry edges over steak to enclose, and place seam side down on a rimmed baking sheet. Repeat for remaining steaks. Cover steaks and refrigerate for 1 hour or until next day.

Bake, uncovered, on lowest rack of a 425° oven for 10 minutes, then move pan to highest rack and bake 8 to 10 minutes longer or until pastry is golden brown.

Serve at once (meat will be rare) and pass the

béarnaise cream sauce to spoon over each steak. Makes 6 servings.

Béarnaise Cream Sauce. Cut ½ small **onion** in chunks. Using metal blade, process with on-off bursts until finely chopped. Place onion in a small pan with 1 tablespoon **wine vinegar** and ¼ teaspoon **tarragon.** Change to slicing disc and slice ¼ pound **mushrooms.**

Boil onion-vinegar mixture over medium heat, stirring, until liquid is evaporated. Add ¼ cup **butter** or margarine and sliced mushrooms. Cook until mushrooms are lightly browned. Pour in ¼ cup **whipping cream;** bring to boiling.

Beat 2 **egg yolks** lightly with a fork. Stir some of hot mixture into egg yolks, then return to pan and cook briefly over low heat, stirring, until thickened slightly. Sauce can be reheated if warmed gently, stirring, over hot (not simmering) water. Makes about 1 cup sauce.

Wine Marinade for Meat

A marinade that flavors and tenderizes meat can help you take advantage of good meat bargains. With a few simple flavor additions, the same basic marinade recipe can be used for beef or lamb, producing a different taste each time.

>   3 cloves garlic
>   2 large onions
>   1½ teaspoons salt
>   1 teaspoon pepper
>   ⅛ teaspoon cayenne
>   ½ cup red wine vinegar
>   1 cup dry red wine

Using metal blade, process garlic until chopped. Cut onion in chunks, add to garlic, and process until puréed. Add salt, pepper, cayenne, wine vinegar, and wine and process for 3 seconds to blend. Cover tightly and store in refrigerator for as long as a month. Makes about 3 cups.

Barbecued Chuck Steak. Buy a **chuck roast** cut about 1½ inches thick and weighing 3½ to 4½ pounds. Treat with **unseasoned meat tenderizer** as directed on package; place meat in a close-fitting baking dish. To ¾ cup **wine marinade for meat,** stir in ½ cup **salad oil,** 1 teaspoon *each* dry **rosemary** and **Worcestershire,** ¼ teaspoon crushed **bay leaf,** and 1 tablespoon **Dijon mustard.** Pour marinade over meat. Cover and refrigerate for 2 to 6 hours, turning occasionally.

Lift meat from marinade; reserve marinade. Place meat on grill 4 to 6 inches above a bed of low-glowing coals. (Or you can place meat on broiler pan about 6 inches from heat). Cook, turning and basting meat with reserved marinade, until done to your liking (takes 30 to 35 minutes for medium rare). Slice diagonally and serve. Makes about 6 servings.

Grilled Lamb Steaks. Slash fat on edges of 4 large **lamb steaks** (about 2½ lbs. total) cut from leg or shoulder, and arrange in a shallow dish. To ¾ cup **wine marinade for meat,** stir in ¼ cup **salad oil,** 1 clove **garlic** (minced or pressed), 1 teaspoon **oregano** leaves, and 2 tablespoons **lemon juice.** Pour over meat, cover and refrigerate for about 2 hours.

Lift steaks from marinade, scraping off excess, and reserve. Either barbecue steaks on a barbecue grill 4 to 6 inches above a bed of low-glowing coals or oven broil about 3 inches from heat. Cook, turning once and brushing with marinade, until brown and done to your liking (takes 8 to 12 minutes for medium rare). Makes 4 servings.

Singapore Satay

Visitors to Southeast Asia soon discover the popular streetside snack known as *satay.* Bite-size pieces of lamb or beef are threaded on skewers, quickly cooked over hot coals, then rolled in a spicy sweet-hot peanut sauce and nibbled off the skewers a bite at a time. It's best to cook satay in successive batches so you can eat it hot from the grill.

>   3 pounds lean boneless beef (sirloin or top
>   round) or lamb (shoulder or leg), or a
>   mixture of both
>   4 cloves garlic
>   ½ cup *each* salad oil and soy sauce
>   2 tablespoons *each* curry powder and sugar
>   Peanut sauce (recipe follows)

Cut meat into ¾-inch cubes. (If you use more than one kind of meat, put each in its own plastic bag.) Using metal blade, process garlic until chopped. Add oil, soy, curry powder, and sugar; process for 3 seconds to blend, then pour over meat cubes (pouring into each plastic bag if you used more than one kind of meat). Marinate in refrigerator for at least 4 hours or as long as 2 days.

Thread meat on long sturdy bamboo skewers (use only one kind of meat on each skewer). Grill meat about 2 inches above a solid bed of medium-hot coals for 8 to 10 minutes, turning frequently, until meat is done to your liking. Roll skewered meat in peanut sauce before eating. Makes 6 to 8 servings.

Peanut Sauce. Using metal blade, process 1 cup **salted Spanish peanuts** until finely chopped but not powdered; set aside. Cut 1 large **onion** in chunks. Process with 2 cloves **garlic,** 1 to 2 tablespoons **chili powder,** 2 teaspoons **ground coriander,** and 1 teaspoon **ground cumin** until puréed.

(Continued on page 35)

ONION-CAPPED French Cheeseburger (page 36) and hot, crispy American Potato Chips (page 51) are products of food processor's slicing and chopping abilities. German beer caps international meal.

Mexican Buffet for Twelve

Many Mexican meals call for a variety of dishes served at one time—which usually means a lot of slicing and chopping. Our Mexican buffet for 12 is no exception, yet the time-consuming steps — preparing the vegetables, fruits, cheese, even refried beans — are all accomplished easily by a food processor.

Guacamole

(Avocado Dip)

Offered here as an appetizer, this Mexican favorite can also be used as a sauce for meats and main dishes, as a dressing for salads, or as a filling for tortillas.

    1 can (4 oz.) whole California green chiles
    2 large ripe avocados
    2 to 3 tablespoons lemon or lime juice
       Salt and pepper
       About ½ teaspoon ground coriander
          (optional)
       Dash of liquid hot pepper seasoning or
          cayenne (optional)

Using metal blade, process chiles with on-off bursts until coarsely chopped. Peel avocados, remove pits, and cut into chunks. Distribute over chiles and process with on-off bursts until mashed. Stir in lemon juice, salt, pepper, and other seasonings to taste. Serve with tortilla chips to dip. Makes about 1⅔ cups.

Ensalada de Nochebuena

(Christmas Eve Salad)

This traditional holiday salad is a delightful combination of fresh fruits and beets; a tart French dressing complements the flavors.

    4 *each* red apples, oranges, and bananas
    1 fresh pineapple or 1 can (1 lb. 14 oz.)
          pineapple chunks, drained
    1 cup orange juice
    1 head iceberg lettuce
    1 jar (1 lb.) whole pickled beets, drained
    1 cup peanuts
    ¼ cup sugar (optional)
       Seeds of 2 pomegranates
       Tart French dressing (¾ cup oil, ¼ cup red
          wine vinegar, about ½ teaspoon salt)

Core unpeeled apples and cut in quarters. Peel oranges, remove white membranes, and cut in quarters. Peel bananas; then peel, quarter, and core pineapple. Using slicing disc, slice each fruit separately. To prevent darkening, pour ⅓ cup of the orange juice over each fruit except pineapple.

Slice lettuce and reserve, then slice beets. Rinse processor bowl and reassemble with metal blade. Process peanuts until coarsely chopped.

To assemble salad, put lettuce in bottom of large shallow bowl. Drain fruits and arrange attractively over lettuce — perhaps with a ring of oranges around the outer edge, a smaller ring of beets inside, then bananas, apples, and finally pineapple in center. Sprinkle with sugar, if you choose to use it. Scatter pomegranate seeds and chopped nuts over all. (At this point, you can cover and chill as long as 2 hours.)

Just before serving, pour on French dressing. Makes 12 servings.

Enchiladas Verdes

(Green Enchiladas)

The creamy sauce covering these cheese-filled enchiladas is very mild, making them a good choice for the tender-mouthed.

    12 ounces jack cheese
     2 large onions
     1 tablespoon salad oil
    ¼ teaspoon salt
       Salad oil
     1 dozen corn tortillas
     2 green onions
    ½ package (10 or 12 oz. size) frozen spinach,
          cooked and drained, or ½ cup fresh,
          chopped, cooked, and drained spinach
     1 can (4 oz.) whole California green chiles,
          seeds removed
     1 can (10¾ oz.) condensed cream of chicken
          soup, undiluted
     1 cup sour cream

Insert shredding disc; shred cheese and set aside. With a knife, cut onions in chunks. Switch to metal blade and process onion with on-off bursts until coarsely chopped. Heat the 1 tablespoon oil in a wide frying pan over medium heat. Add onion and cook until soft (about 5 minutes). Stir in the salt.

In a small frying pan, heat ½ inch oil over medium heat. One at a time, dip tortillas in oil for a few seconds on each side or just until soft. Sprinkle 2 tablespoons *each* cooked onion and cheese across the middle of each tortilla and roll to enclose. Place tortillas, seam side down, in a shallow, greased 9 by 13-inch baking pan.

Cut green onions and part of tops into 1-inch lengths. Process until chopped. Add spinach, chiles, soup, and sour cream and process until puréed. Spoon sauce over tortillas and sprinkle remaining cheese over all.

To serve, bake, uncovered, in a 350° oven for 30 minutes or until hot and bubbly. Makes 12 servings.

Tostadas

A whole crisp-fried tortilla on a bed of shredded lettuce forms the bottom layer of a tostada. Then refried beans, cheese, meat, and garnishes — tomatoes, onions, guacamole, and sour cream — are piled high. Let guests help themselves to ingredients.

```
2   heads iceberg lettuce
1   pound jack or Cheddar cheese
3   large tomatoes
2   medium-size onions
    Salad oil
1   dozen corn tortillas
2   cups refried beans, heated (recipe follows)
2   cups ground beef filling, heated (recipe
      follows)
    Guacamole (recipe at left)
    Sour cream
1   can (7 oz.) red or green chile salsa
```

Insert slicing disc; slice lettuce and place in individual serving dish. Change to shredding disc; shred cheese and place in individual serving dish. Cut tomatoes and onions in chunks. Change to metal blade and process tomatoes and onions separately with on-off bursts until coarsely chopped. Place in individual serving dishes.

In a wide frying pan, heat ½ inch salad oil over medium heat. Fry tortillas, one at a time, using a spatula or tongs to turn tortilla frequently (or to hold it under oil) until it is crisp, slightly puffed, and lightly browned (about 1 minute or less). Drain on paper towels; then stack on a serving plate and cover to keep warm.

For each tostada, spread a layer of shredded lettuce over a dinner plate. Add a fried tortilla. Spread with about 3 or 4 tablespoons refried beans, sprinkle with cheese, cover with 2 or 3 tablespoons ground beef filling, and top with ¼ cup more shredded lettuce. Garnish with a spoonful of tomatoes, onions, guacamole, a dollop of sour cream, and chile salsa. Makes 12 servings.

Refried Beans. Wash and drain 1 pound of **dried pinto or pink beans.** Combine with about 5 cups **water** in a 3-quart pan and bring to a boil. Cover, cook for 2 minutes, then remove from heat and let stand for 1 hour.

Peel 1 or 2 large **onions** and cut into chunks. Using metal blade, process with on-off bursts until coarsely chopped. Add to beans and return to heat.

Bring to a boil, reduce heat, and simmer, adding more water if necessary, until beans are tender (about 2 hours). Drain thoroughly.

Using metal blade, process beans, ½ at a time, until mashed. Return to pan; add ½ to 1 cup **bacon drippings,** margarine, or lard, and cook, stirring often, until beans are thickened and very hot. Add **salt** and **pepper** to taste. Serve hot or reheat.

Ground Beef Filling. Heat 2 tablespoons **salad oil** in wide frying pan over medium heat; add 2 pounds **lean ground beef,** and cook until brown and crumbly.

Peel and cut 2 medium-size **onions** in chunks. Using metal blade, process onion with on-off bursts until finely chopped. Add to meat and cook until limp (about 4 minutes). Discard excess pan drippings. Add 1 can (10 oz.) **enchilada sauce,** ½ teaspoon *each* **ground cumin** and **oregano leaves,** and 1 to 2 teaspoons **chili powder.** Cook, stirring occasionally, for 10 minutes; then boil rapidly until most of liquid has evaporated. Serve hot or reheat.

Crema de Mango
(Mango Cream)

Here's a sweet fruit dessert that looks quite festive when served in a decorative pottery bowl or individual dishes.

```
1   cup blanched almonds
2   oranges, peeled (white membrane
      removed) and seeded
5   large ripe mangoes or 2 cans (15 oz. each)
      mangoes, drained
¼   cup sugar
1   tablespoon lemon juice
2   cups whipping cream
    Green maraschino cherries (optional)
```

Using metal blade, process almonds with on-off bursts until coarsely chopped; set aside. Section oranges; cut sections in half and set aside. Peel mangoes, cut into pieces, and process until mashed. Transfer to a bowl. Add sugar to taste (up to ¼ cup). Stir in orange pieces and lemon juice.

Whip cream and fold into mango mixture; add almonds. Pour into large bowl or individual dishes and garnish with cherries, if desired. Chill. Makes 12 servings.

Pineapple Cream. Prepare Crema de Mango, substituting puréed pineapple for the mashed mango. Peel 1 **pineapple,** cut in chunks, and cut away core. (Or use 2 cans, about 1 lb. *each,* drained pineapple chunks.) Using metal blade, process pineapple, ½ at a time, until puréed. Sweeten with ¼ to ½ cup sugar.

Heat 2 tablespoons **salad oil** in a wide frying pan over medium heat. Add onion mixture and cook, stirring occasionally, for 5 minutes. Reduce heat to low and add peanuts. Gradually stir in 1 can (12 oz.) frozen **coconut milk,** thawed; 3 tablespoons packed **brown sugar;** and 2 tablespoons *each* **lemon juice** and **soy sauce.** Cook, uncovered, just below simmering (do not boil), stirring occasionally, until sauce thickens (about 15 minutes).

Serve warm or at room temperature in wide, shallow, rimmed dishes — use 2 or 3 dishes for serving convenience. Makes 2½ cups.

Ham and Apple Burgers

For a quick lunch or supper, turn leftover ham into a fruit-flavored meal in a bun.

- 3 cups cooked ham (cut in 1½-inch chunks to measure)
- 1 large tart green apple
- 2 stalks celery
- ½ small onion
- ½ small green pepper, seeded
- 2 tablespoons butter or margarine
- 8 hamburger buns
- 1 tablespoon Dijon mustard
- ½ cup sour cream

Using metal blade, process ham, ½ at a time, with 3 or 4 long bursts or until coarsely chopped; set aside. Peel, quarter, and core apple. Cut celery, onion, and pepper in chunks. Process apple and vegetables together with 4 or 5 on-off bursts or until coarsely chopped. Melt butter in a wide frying pan over medium heat. Add apple mixture and cook, stirring, for 2 minutes. Add ham and cook for 5 minutes.

Meanwhile, place buns, cut side up, on a cooky sheet. Broil 3 inches from heat until lightly toasted.

Stir mustard into ham mixture. Remove pan from heat and stir in sour cream. Spoon ham mixture onto bottom half of each bun; cover with top half. Makes 8 sandwiches.

Glazed Barbecued Spareribs

The fruit-based glaze in this recipe burns easily, so don't use it when you start to cook the meat. Wait until the meat is nearly done, then begin the basting to add flavor and color.

SAVORY ITALIAN HERBS flavor Meat Loaf in a Bread Basket (page 29); Cream of Cauliflower Soup (page 21) makes a perfect accompaniment on a brisk fall day.

- 1 clove garlic
- 1 can (1 lb.) cling peach halves, drained; or 3 large peaches, peeled, pitted, and halved
- ¼ cup *each* salad oil and honey
- ⅓ cup soy sauce
- 2 tablespoons packed brown sugar
- ¼ teaspoon ground ginger
- 1 teaspoon sesame seed
- 3 to 4 pounds lean pork spareribs

Using metal blade, process garlic until chopped. Add peaches and process until puréed. Add oil, honey, soy, brown sugar, ginger, and sesame seed; process for 3 seconds to blend. Trim excess fat from spareribs.

To barbecue, place meat on grill 4 to 6 inches above a bed of low-glowing coals. Cook for 45 minutes, turning about every 10 minutes. Add briquets if needed to maintain a constant heat.

After 45 minutes, begin basting ribs with peach mixture and cook for about 20 minutes longer, basting and turning frequently, until ribs are browned and meat is tender when pierced.

Cover any unused glaze and store in refrigerator for as long as 2 weeks. Makes 4 to 6 servings.

Alsatian-style Ham

All the juices and natural sweetness from finely chopped vegetables mingle with ham as it simmers very slowly in the colorful sauce.

- 1 clove garlic
- 1 medium-size onion
- 1 small carrot
- 1 medium-size turnip
- 1 tablespoon butter or margarine
  Leaves from 2 inside stalks of celery
- ½ cup *each* dry white wine and water
  Dash of liquid hot pepper seasoning
- ½ cup packed parsley sprigs
- 2 to 2½ pound piece cooked boneless ham
- 2 teaspoons cornstarch
- 1 tablespoon water
- 1 teaspoon sugar
- ½ teaspoon *each* prepared mustard and horseradish

Using metal blade, process garlic until chopped. Cut onion in chunks, add to garlic, and process with on-off bursts until finely chopped. Turn into a heavy 4-quart pan. Cut carrot and turnip in chunks and process together until finely chopped. Add to onion along with butter; cook, stirring occasionally, over medium heat until onion is soft but not browned (about 5 minutes). Process celery leaves with on-off bursts until finely chopped. Add to onion mixture along with wine, water, and hot pepper seasoning. Simmer, uncovered, for 10 minutes. Process parsley until finely chopped; reserve.

(Continued on page 37)

Ground Meat and Sausage from Scratch

There are several good reasons why you may want to process your own meat for hamburger patties, breakfast sausage, or other ground meat dishes.

Start with taste—there's a delicious difference in the flavor of meat that goes directly from processor to pan. What's more, you can be absolutely sure of the quality and freshness of the meat you process yourself. You can keep it as lean as you like, and with sausage, you can adjust the seasonings to suit your own taste.

Many recipes call for small quantities of several different kinds of ground meat—something that is easy for you to process at home, but difficult for meat markets whose commercial-size equipment is geared to grinding large quantities only.

To say you'll "have fun" chopping, cooking, and serving meat may sound like the height of frivolity—but we found that it *is* fun, and that may be the best of all reasons for doing it.

Choosing the Meat... For hamburgers, a super-lean ground beef patty may be your choice, but keep in mind that chopped meat needs *some* fat for tenderness. For that reason, meat from the chuck, which has a fair amount of marbling (internal streaking of fat), is the best cut to use. Buy boneless chuck or bone it yourself, remove connective fibers and heavy outside fat, and cut meat in 1-inch cubes.

You can use leaner, though slightly more expensive, cuts of beef, too—rump roast, cross rib roast, sirloin tip roast, or top round. But because these cuts are lean, you need to make up for the lack of natural fat. Do this by adding 2 tablespoons margarine or salad oil for each cup of meat cubes or by cooking the meat *only* to the rare stage.

...And Chopping It. Using the metal blade, process 1 cup meat cubes at a time with on-off bursts until meat is chopped medium fine. Meat that is too coarse in texture doesn't hold together well in a patty, and meat that is over-processed to the point of being very fine has almost no texture at all.

If you wish to grind pork, veal, or lamb, buy shoulder cuts and bone the meat, or look for boneless pork butt, veal stew meat, or lamb stew meat.

You can reduce the calories in ground beef for patties by combining chopped chuck with tofu (soybean curd). For each pound of meat, mix in ½ pound tofu (drained on paper towels and mashed) before cooking.

To figure amounts, just remember that ½ pound of boneless meat makes 1 cup of meat cubes or about 1 cup of chopped meat.

French Cheeseburger

(Pictured on page 31)

Onion slices, cooked slowly in butter to a golden sweetness, give the French touch to an American favorite.

Process 1½ pounds **boneless chuck** according to preceding directions. Season meat with ½ teaspoon **salt.** Divide meat in 4 parts; shape into ½-inch-thick patties. Broil on a rack 3 inches from heat until cooked to your liking (allow 4 minutes on each side for rare).

While patties are still on broiler, top each with a slice of **jack cheese.** Split 4 **crusty rolls** in half and set on oven rack alongside patties. Broil until rolls are toasted and cheese melts over patties. Put a meat patty on bottom half of each roll, spoon 2 tablespoons **slow-cooked onions** (page 52) on each patty, sprinkle with freshly ground **pepper,** add top half of each roll, and serve. Pass **Dijon mustard.** Makes 4 servings.

Spicy Pork Breakfast Sausage

Bacon adds a smoky flavor but surprisingly little fat to this tasty sausage. Since it is meant to be eaten fresh and contains no preservative, use it within 2 days or freeze for as long as 3 months.

Process 2 pounds boneless **pork butt** or shoulder according to preceding directions; set aside. Without separating slices, cut ½ pound **bacon** crosswise in 4 pieces. (Use bacon directly from the refrigerator; if it stands at room temperature it becomes too soft to process.)

Using metal blade, process bacon with 3 long bursts or until finely chopped. Add to bacon 1¾ teaspoons **rubbed sage,** ½ teaspoon **ground nutmeg,** ⅛ teaspoon **cayenne,** ½ teaspoon *each* **salt** and **pepper,** and ¼ cup **cold water;** process with 1 on-off burst to blend. Add to chopped pork and mix well. Shape into 3 rolls, *each* 6 inches long and 2 inches in diameter. Wrap in plastic wrap and refrigerate.

To cook sausage, cut in ½-inch-thick slices and fry slowly over medium heat (adding a little **butter** or margarine if meat sticks to pan) for 5 minutes on each side or until nicely browned. Makes 2½ pounds sausage.

Place ham in pan with liquid; cover and simmer over low heat for 1 hour or until ham is very tender when pierced. Transfer ham to a serving platter.

Skim fat from pan juices. Mix cornstarch and water; add to pan juices along with parsley, sugar, mustard, and horseradish. Cook over medium heat, stirring, until sauce is slightly thickened. Serve separately to spoon over meat. Makes 6 to 8 servings.

Venezuelan Barbecued Pork

(Pictured on page 39)

Because pork butt has a fair amount of fat mixed through the lean, it remains moist and juicy when barbecued. This recipe tells you how to butterfly the meat to make a thick rectangular steak that's easy to carve. You marinate the pork in a tangy mixture that doubles as a basting and serving sauce.

    3- pound boneless pork butt, approximately 9
        inches long, 4 inches wide, and 3 inches
        thick
 ⅔ cup packed parsley sprigs
 1 to 2 cloves garlic
 1 medium-size onion
 1 small red bell or green pepper, seeded
 ½ cup white vinegar
 ¼ cup salad oil
 1½ teaspoons salt
 ¼ teaspoon pepper

Trim heavy outside fat from meat. Split meat lengthwise through the thickness to within ½ inch of the other side, then open up meat so it forms a steak 1½ inches thick (or have meat butterflied at the market). Place meat, fat side down, on working surface. Score top of meat with 3 lengthwise and 5 crosswise cuts, making each cut about ½ inch deep. Place meat in a baking pan, scored side up.

Using metal blade, process parsley until finely chopped; transfer to a bowl. Process garlic until chopped. Cut onion and red pepper in chunks, add to garlic, and process with on-off bursts until finely chopped. Add chopped vegetables to parsley along with white vinegar, oil, salt, and pepper. Mix together, then pour over meat. Cover and refrigerate for at least 2 hours or until next day.

In a covered barbecue, ignite 40 long-burning briquets and let them burn down until covered with ash (30 to 40 minutes). Bank 20 coals on each side and place a drip pan (or fashion one from heavy-duty foil) in center.

Lift meat from marinade and drain briefly, reserving marinade. Place meat on grill, scored side down, directly over drip pan, 4 to 6 inches above coals. Adjust dampers to maintain a low heat and add briquets as needed to keep heat constant. Cook meat on 1 side for 40 minutes, then turn and insert a meat thermometer into thickest portion. Cook about 40 minutes longer or until thermometer reaches 170°. Baste meat frequently with marinade while cooking.

To serve, cut in thin slices. Heat remaining marinade and serve as a sauce. Makes 6 to 8 servings.

Pork with Red Cabbage

Cooked in the French manner, pork, cabbage, and apples, braised in red wine, make a complete meal.

    3 cloves garlic
    2 teaspoons salt
 ¾ teaspoon thyme leaves
 ¼ teaspoon *each* pepper and ground allspice
 2½ to 3-pound pork loin roast, boned, rolled
        and tied
    1 small onion
    1 medium-size carrot
    5 tablespoons butter or margarine
    2 tart green apples
    1 medium-size head (about 2 lbs.) red cabbage
    2 tablespoons vinegar
 ⅛ teaspoon ground nutmeg
    1 tablespoon salad oil
    1 cup dry red wine
    1 bay leaf

Mince 1 clove of the garlic; mix with salt, thyme, pepper, and allspice. Rub over meat. Cover and refrigerate for at least 2 hours or until next day.

Using metal blade, process remaining 2 cloves garlic until chopped. Cut onion and carrot in chunks. Add onion to garlic and process with on-off bursts until coarsely chopped. Turn into a 5 to 6-quart kettle. Process carrot until finely chopped. Add to onion along with 4 tablespoons of the butter, and, stirring occasionally, cook over medium-low heat until vegetables are soft but not browned (about 5 minutes).

Quarter and core unpeeled apples. Process with on-off bursts until chopped; set aside. Change to slicing disc. Cut cabbage in wedges to fit feed tube; slice. Add apples and cabbage to onion mixture and, stirring, cook until cabbage is slightly limp. Add vinegar and nutmeg. Spoon mixture into a 5 to 6-quart casserole.

In kettle, heat remaining 1 tablespoon butter with salad oil over medium heat. Add seasoned pork roast and brown well on all sides. Then, in casserole, make a well in center of cabbage large enough to hold roast, and place meat in the well. Insert meat thermometer in thickest part of roast.

In a pan, combine wine and bay leaf; bring to boil and pour over meat. Bake, covered, in a 325° oven for about 2 hours or until thermometer registers 170°. Transfer meat to a platter and lift vegetables onto platter with a slotted spoon. Keep meat warm while you rapidly boil juices down to about 1 cup.

To serve, cut meat into ½-inch slices and pass sauce to spoon individually onto meat and cabbage. Makes 5 or 6 servings.

Stuffed Veal Rolls

Slices of veal, pounded thin, are filled with an herb and bacon stuffing. The rolls are braised, and a flavorful sauce is made with the pan juices.

    1   to 1¼ pounds boneless veal (cut from the
         leg), cut ¼ inch thick
    ½   pound bacon
    1   clove garlic
    ¼   cup packed parsley sprigs
    ¼   teaspoon *each* tarragon, dry basil, thyme
         leaves, and dry rosemary
    2   tablespoons butter or margarine
    3   sprigs parsley
    ½   small onion
    ½   small green pepper, seeded
    ½   cup regular-strength chicken broth
    ¼   cup dry white wine
    ¼   teaspoon thyme leaves
    ⅛   teaspoon pepper
    ½   small bay leaf
    1   teaspoon cornstarch
    1   tablespoon water

Trim connective tissue and any fat from meat. Place meat between 2 sheets of plastic wrap, allowing several inches between pieces. Pound meat gently but firmly with a flat-surfaced mallet until meat is about ¹/₁₆ inch thick. Following natural division of meat as much as possible, cut into rectangles about 4 by 6 inches. (Some pieces may be slightly smaller because of the original shape of the meat.)

Without separating slices, cut bacon crosswise in 4 sections. (Use bacon directly from refrigerator; if it stands at room temperature it becomes too soft to process.) Using metal blade, process bacon with 3 long bursts or until finely chopped; set aside.

Process garlic until chopped. Add the ¼ cup parsley, tarragon, basil, thyme, and rosemary; process until parsley is finely chopped. Distribute bacon over parsley mixture and process with 1 long burst.

Place about 1 tablespoon of this mixture on each pounded piece of veal and spread to within ½ inch of edges. Fold ⅓ of narrow side over onto filling, then fold other side over onto first side. Secure the 3 open edges with wooden picks.

Melt butter in a wide frying pan over medium heat. Add meat and brown evenly on all sides, turning as needed.

Process the 3 sprigs parsley until finely chopped. Cut onion and green pepper in chunks; add to parsley and process with on-off bursts until finely chopped. Add to meat and cook over medium heat

for 2 minutes. Add broth, wine, thyme, pepper, and bay leaf. Bring to a boil, then reduce heat, cover, and simmer very gently for about 25 minutes or until meat is fork tender. Place veal on a serving platter, remove picks, and keep meat warm.

Remove bay leaf from cooking liquid. Blend cornstarch and water. Bring cooking liquid to a boil, add cornstarch mixture, and stir until sauce is thickened (about 30 seconds). Pour hot sauce over meat and serve. Makes 4 servings.

Stuffed Breast of Veal

What breast of veal lacks in meatiness is made up for by the savory meat stuffing. If you like, skim and discard fat from the pan juices, bring them to a boil, then thicken as much as you like and serve as a sauce with the meat.

    1   clove garlic
    1   medium-size onion
    2   tablespoons olive oil or salad oil
    ½   pound lean ground beef
    ½   pound mushrooms
    1   package (10 or 12 oz.) frozen chopped
         spinach, thawed
    2   eggs
    ½   teaspoon *each* salt and dry basil
    4   ounces jack cheese
    2½   to 3-pound veal breast, split to form a
         pocket for stuffing
    1   cup regular-strength beef broth

Using metal blade, process garlic until chopped. Cut onion in chunks, add to garlic, and process with on-off bursts until coarsely chopped. Heat oil in a wide frying pan over medium heat. Add onion and garlic and, stirring, cook for 2 minutes. Add beef and cook until browned and crumbly.

Process mushrooms, ½ at a time, with on-off bursts until coarsely chopped. Squeeze spinach with your hands to press out all liquid. Add mushrooms and spinach to meat and, stirring, cook for 5 minutes or until all liquid has evaporated; let cool. Process eggs with salt and basil for 3 seconds; stir into meat mixture. Change to shredding disc; shred cheese, then stir into meat mixture.

Pack stuffing into veal breast; bring edges together and fasten securely with small skewers, or sew with string to hold stuffing inside. Place meat, stuffing side up, in a roasting pan. Pour in beef broth. Cover pan and bake in a 325° oven for 2 hours; remove cover and bake for about 30 minutes longer to brown surface. Remove skewers or string and slice between bones to serve. Makes 4 to 6 servings.

WAIT UNTIL DUSK on a hot summer day to serve this Venezuelan Barbecued Pork (page 37) with its tangy marinade-sauce. Accompany with Barbecue-style Beans (page 51).

Fish & Poultry

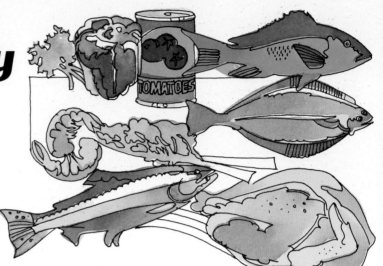

All by themselves, fish and poultry are highly satisfactory foods. But pamper them with an unusual sauce, coating, topping, seasoning, or stuffing and they're transformed into exceptionally good-looking and good-tasting entrées. On the next eight pages are recipes that guide you through these transformations, with your food processor doing much of the work. The results are fish and poultry dishes with a fresh new look and taste—proof that there's almost no end to what you can do with these two food basics.

Shrimp Curry in a Hurry

Serving a number of condiments with this curry makes it a festive dish. They can be prepared swiftly and easily with your food processor.

You can assemble this curry ahead of time, but do not heat it until just before serving. The vegetables should still be crisp-tender.

- 1 large stalk celery
- 1 can (8 oz.) water chestnuts, drained
- 1 small onion
- ½ medium-size green pepper
- 1 large green apple
- 1 clove garlic
- 4 tablespoons salad oil
- 1 pound medium-size shrimp, shelled and deveined
- 2 to 3 teaspoons curry powder
- ¼ teaspoon ground ginger
- 2 tablespoons *each* Worcestershire and dry sherry
- 2 cans (10¾ oz. *each*) condensed cream of mushroom soup, undiluted
- 1½ to 2 cups rice, cooked
  Condiments: Chutney, chopped peanuts, chopped hard-cooked eggs, chopped crisp-fried bacon, and chopped onion

Cut celery in lengths to fit feed tube. Insert slicing disc in food processor and slice celery and water chestnuts; transfer to a bowl. Cut onion in chunks. Cut green pepper in chunks and discard seeds. Peel, quarter, and core apple. Switch to metal blade and process garlic until chopped. Add onion and process with on-off bursts until onion is coarsely chopped; add to celery mixture. Process green pepper and apple separately with on-off bursts until coarsely chopped; add to celery mixture.

Heat 2 tablespoons of the oil in a wide frying pan over medium-high heat. Add shrimp and, stirring, cook for 3 minutes or until shrimp turn pink. Stir in curry powder, ginger, Worcestershire, and sherry and cook for 1 minute; remove from pan.

Heat remaining 2 tablespoons oil in same pan. Add chopped vegetable mixture and cook over high heat, stirring, for 3 minutes or until tender-crisp. Stir in mushroom soup and shrimp mixture. Heat through and serve over rice. Serve condiments in separate bowls. Makes 4 or 5 servings.

Cheesy Fish Sticks

In this recipe, you can experiment with different types of firm cheese, but it is important to follow the sequence of steps when making the coating. Processing the shredded cheese with dry bread crumbs ensures that the cheese remains crumbled and not creamed.

- 4 ounces sharp Cheddar cheese
- 4 slices crisp dry bread
- ⅓ cup salad oil
- ½ teaspoon salt
- 1 clove garlic, minced or pressed
- 2 pounds white fish fillets (halibut, turbot, rockfish, sea bass), ¾ inch thick

Using shredding disc, shred cheese; set aside. Change to metal blade. Break bread in pieces and process to make fine crumbs; you should have 1 cup. Distribute shredded cheese over crumbs in processor bowl, and process until mixture looks like cornmeal. Turn out on a piece of wax paper.

In a bowl combine salad oil, salt, and garlic. Cut fillets widthwise in 1½-inch-wide pieces. Dip each piece of fish in seasoned oil, then coat on both sides with cheese mixture. Arrange in single layer, without crowding, in a lightly greased baking pan. Bake in a 450° oven for 8 to 12 minutes or until fish flakes easily when probed in thickest part with a fork. Makes 4 to 6 servings.

Cheese-broiled Fish Fillets

Fillets (flat pieces) of halibut, salmon, swordfish, rockfish, sole, or turbot are all savory when cooked this easy way.

    2   green onions
    ¼   cup butter or margarine
    3   tablespoons mayonnaise
    ½   cup grated Parmesan cheese
        Dash of liquid hot pepper seasoning
    2   pounds fish fillets, ½ to ¾ inch thick
    2   tablespoons lemon juice

Cut green onions and part of tops in 1-inch lengths. Using metal blade, process until chopped. Cut butter in chunks, add to onions, and process until creamy. Add mayonnaise, cheese, and hot pepper seasoning; process for 3 seconds to blend.

Arrange fillets in a single layer in a well-greased shallow baking pan. Brush with lemon juice and let stand for 10 minutes. Broil about 5 inches from heat until fish flakes easily when probed in the thickest part with a fork (6 to 8 minutes). Remove from heat and spread cheese and onion mixture over fish. Return to heat and broil until topping is bubbly (about 2 minutes). With a spatula, transfer fillets to a warm serving plate. Makes 4 to 6 servings.

Baked Sole, Duxelles

A special seasoning called *duxelles* — made from minced mushrooms—flavors this simple presentation of sole. You might serve it with buttered new potatoes and asparagus.

    1   tablespoon *each* salad oil and all-purpose
        flour
    1   cup packed parsley sprigs
    ½   cup duxelles (page 50)
    ¾   teaspoon tarragon
    ⅓   cup dry white wine or regular-strength
        chicken broth
    ¼   cup whipping cream
    1½ pounds sole fillets
        Salt, pepper, and paprika
    3   slices firm white bread
    3   tablespoons butter or margarine

Spread oil over bottom of a baking dish approximately 9 by 13 inches. Sprinkle flour evenly over oil.

Using metal blade, process parsley until finely chopped; remove half the parsley and reserve. Distribute duxelles over remaining parsley; add tarragon and process with 2 on-off bursts to mix. Sprinkle mixture over bottom of prepared baking dish. Drizzle with wine and cream. Season fillets lightly with salt, pepper, and paprika and arrange on top of duxelles so fillets overlap only slightly.

Tear bread into quarters and process to make soft crumbs. Melt butter in a frying pan, add crumbs, and, stirring occasionally, cook over medium heat until lightly toasted (about 5 minutes). Remove from heat, stir in reserved parsley, and sprinkle over fish. (At this point, you can cover and refrigerate until ready to bake.)

Bake, uncovered, in a 350° oven for 20 minutes (25 minutes if refrigerated) or until fish flakes easily when probed in thickest part with a fork. Makes 4 to 6 servings.

Cioppino

(Pictured on page 42)

Cioppino is a cross between a soup and a stew. It's fast to prepare because the various shellfish cook in their shells. And it's messy to eat because you must pick up the shellfish with your fingers if you want to enjoy their succulent flavor. But that's the fun of this dish that is so good for an informal party. Serve it with a green salad and offer French bread to absorb the delicious sauce.

    1   medium-size onion
    1   large red bell or green pepper
    ½   bunch (½ lb.) Swiss chard
    2   cloves garlic
    ½   cup packed parsley sprigs
    1½ teaspoons *each* marjoram leaves and dry
        basil
    ¾   teaspoon *each* dry rosemary, sage leaves,
        and thyme leaves
    1½ dozen clams in the shell
    1   large cooked crab, cleaned and cracked
    1   pound medium-size shrimp
    1   pound sea bass, rockfish, or other
        firm-fleshed white fish fillets
    1   large can (1 lb. 12 oz.) tomatoes
    1   can (6 oz.) tomato paste
    ¼   cup olive oil or salad oil
    1   teaspoon salt
    ½   teaspoon freshly ground pepper
    ½   cup dry white wine

Cut onion in chunks. Cut red pepper in chunks and discard seeds. Cut Swiss chard stems in 2-inch lengths; cut leaves in 2-inch-wide strips. Using metal blade, process onion, red pepper, Swiss chard stems, and leaves separately with on-off bursts until each is coarsely chopped. Transfer each vegetable to the same bowl after it is chopped.

(Continued on page 43)

Process garlic until chopped. Add parsley, marjoram, basil, rosemary, sage, and thyme, and process until parsley is finely chopped. Mix with chopped vegetables.

Scrub clams and arrange in bottom of a heavy 8-quart kettle. Sprinkle ⅓ of vegetable mixture over clams. Put cracked crab in next and sprinkle with another ⅓ of the vegetables. Wash shrimp and place on top of crab and vegetables, then cover with remaining ⅓ vegetable mixture. Cut fish fillets in 1-inch strips and arrange on top.

Still using metal blade, process tomatoes and their liquid, tomato paste, oil, salt, and pepper with 2 on-off bursts, or until tomatoes are coarsely chopped; pour over fish. Cover kettle, bring to a boil, reduce heat, and simmer for 30 minutes; pour in wine and simmer 10 minutes longer. Serve in big soup bowls with plenty of sauce. Be sure to dip down to bottom of kettle for clams. Makes 6 main-dish servings.

Scallops and Mushrooms au Gratin

You can prepare these creamy scallops and mushrooms ahead of time and serve as an entrée or first course.

    1   pound scallops, cut in bite-size pieces
    1   cup regular-strength chicken broth
    ½   pound mushrooms
    3   tablespoons butter or margarine
    1½ teaspoons lemon juice
    1   small onion
    3   tablespoons all-purpose flour
    ¼   cup whipping cream
        Dash of nutmeg
    ¼   cup packed parsley sprigs
    3   ounces Swiss cheese
        Salt

Combine scallops and broth in a small pan. Bring to a boil, cover, reduce heat, and simmer for 5 minutes or until scallops are opaque. Let cool in broth. Drain and reserve broth; you should have 1 cup. If not, add more chicken broth to make 1 cup.

Insert slicing disc in food processor; slice mushrooms. Melt 1½ tablespoons of the butter in a wide frying pan; add mushrooms and lemon juice. Cook, stirring, on medium-high heat until mushrooms are lightly browned and all liquid is evaporated; transfer to a bowl.

Cut onion into chunks. Switch to metal blade and process onion with on-off bursts until finely

chopped. Place onion in frying pan with remaining 1½ tablespoons butter and cook, stirring, over medium heat until onion is limp but not browned. Stir in flour. Remove pan from heat and blend in reserved scallop broth. Return to heat and bring to a boil, stirring; cook until thickened. Add mushrooms, cream, and nutmeg. Remove from heat.

Process parsley until finely chopped; set aside. Change to shredding disc and shred cheese; you should have ¾ cup. Stir parsley, ¼ cup of the cheese, and reserved scallops into sauce. Season to taste with salt. Divide mixture evenly among 3 individual casseroles or 6 purchased scallop shells and sprinkle remaining ½ cup cheese evenly over surfaces. (At this point you may cover and refrigerate until next day.)

Bake, uncovered, in a 400° oven for about 12 minutes (15 minutes if chilled) or until hot and bubbling. Makes 3 main-dish servings or 6 first-course servings.

Scandinavian Fish Balls or Pudding

Fish balls or fish pudding, often served in Scandinavian countries, is a very versatile dish. You can sauté the basic soufflé-like mixture for feathery light fish cakes, or you can bake it for an even lighter dish. Fish balls are traditionally served with parsley-buttered boiled potatoes; fish pudding is often served with a creamy shrimp sauce.

Start with fresh fish if possible. If you use frozen fish, let it thaw, then dry it thoroughly between paper towels. Potato flour, which is used to give body to the mixture, is available in most supermarkets.

    1   pound boned and skinned salmon or
          halibut
    1½ teaspoons salt
    ¼   teaspoon white pepper
    2   tablespoons *each* all-purpose flour and
          potato flour
    2   cups half-and-half (light cream)
    3   tablespoons butter or margarine
        Shrimp sauce (recipe follows)

Cut fish in 1-inch pieces. Rub each piece with your fingers to feel any bones in meat — they are easy to pull out.

With metal blade in place, turn on food processor. Drop fish pieces, a few at a time, down feed tube and process until fish is mashed. Scrape sides and bottom of processor bowl with a spatula, then process for 30 seconds to make a smooth paste. Sprinkle salt, pepper, flour, and potato flour over fish. Process for 15 seconds to blend. With motor still running, slowly pour 1 cup of the half-and-half down feed tube. Scrape sides and bottom with a spatula, then continue to process, adding remaining 1 cup

CIOPPINO, a lively mélange of fish, shellfish, minced vegetables, and tomatoes, is a cross between soup and stew (page 41).

half-and-half— mixture will look like billowy whipped cream. (At this point you can transfer it to a bowl, cover, and chill for as long as 8 hours.)

To prepare fish balls, melt butter in a wide frying pan over medium-low heat. To shape each fish ball, scoop out 2 tablespoons of the puréed fish mixture with a soup spoon and smooth the top with a knife so it forms an oval; with knife tip, push oval into butter. Cook for 3 minutes on each side or until lightly browned.

To prepare fish pudding, omit the 3 tablespoons butter. Spoon puréed fish mixture into a buttered 9 by 5-inch loaf pan, then bang pan on counter to settle mixture and eliminate air bubbles. Cover tightly with foil and set pan in a larger pan containing at least 1 inch scalding water. Bake in a 350° oven for 30 minutes or until a knife inserted in the middle comes out clean. Cut in slices and serve with shrimp sauce. Makes 6 servings.

Shrimp Sauce. Melt ¼ cup **butter** or margarine in a pan over medium heat. Mix in ¼ cup **all-purpose flour** and cook, stirring, until flour is light golden color. Remove from heat and blend in 2 cups **milk** and ¼ cup **half-and-half** (light cream). Return to heat and, stirring, bring to a full rolling boil. Add ¾ teaspoon **salt,** dash of **white pepper,** 1 teaspoon **lemon juice,** 1 teaspoon **dill weed,** and 1 to 1½ cups small cooked **shrimp.** Serve hot; or cover and refrigerate for as long as 2 days, then reheat. Makes about 2½ cups sauce.

Crusty Baked Chicken

(Picnic-style Chicken pictured on page 47)

Coating chicken with seasoned crumbs and baking it is a delicious way to duplicate fried chicken, but without the mess. Here are three different coatings to use when time is short. Each recipe is enough for one chicken.

Use a 3-pound **broiler-fryer chicken** cut in pieces. Roll pieces in **coating** (recipes follow), then place skin side up, in a lightly greased baking pan, arranging pieces so they do not touch. Bake in a 350° oven for 1 hour or until chicken is no longer pink in thickest part (cut a small gash to test). Makes 4 or 5 servings.

Nothing-to-it Chicken. Using metal blade, process 1 package (7 oz.) **seasoned stuffing mix,** ½ of the package at a time, until coarsely crushed. Process with three 2-second bursts. Dip chicken in ¼ cup melted **butter** or margarine, then roll in crumbs and bake as directed above.

Parmesan Chicken. Break 4 slices of crisp, dry **bread** into pieces and, using the metal blade, process pieces to make fine crumbs; you should have 1 cup. Add ½ cup grated **Parmesan cheese,** ½ tea-

spoon *each* **paprika** and **garlic salt,** and a dash of **pepper.** Process 2 seconds to mix. Dip chicken in ¼ cup melted **butter** or margarine, then roll in crumbs and bake as directed above.

Picnic-style Chicken. Using metal blade, process 4 cups **cornflakes,** 2 cups at a time, to make coarse crumbs. Process with three 2-second bursts. Season ⅓ cup **mayonnaise** with ½ teaspoon *each* **salt, garlic salt,** and crushed dry **rosemary.** Coat chicken with mayonnaise mixture, then roll in crumbs and bake as directed above.

Chicken Cacciatore

In the Italian style, chicken develops rich flavor as it simmers in a vegetable-laced tomato sauce. Accompany with parsley-buttered spaghetti or rice.

- 2 tablespoons *each* butter and olive oil
- 3- pound broiler-fryer chicken, cut in pieces
- ½ pound mushrooms
- 1 medium-size onion
- 2 green peppers
- 2 cloves garlic
- ¼ cup packed parsley sprigs
- ½ cup water
- ½ cup dry white wine or chicken broth
- 1 can (6 oz.) tomato paste
- 1½ teaspoons salt
- ¼ teaspoon *each* marjoram, oregano, and thyme leaves
- 1 teaspoon chicken-flavored stock base or 1 chicken bouillon cube

Heat butter and oil in a wide frying pan over medium-high heat. Put in chicken pieces and cook, turning, until browned on all sides; remove from pan and set aside. Pour off and discard all but 3 tablespoons pan drippings.

Meanwhile, slice mushrooms with slicing disc; set aside. Cut onion in chunks; cut green peppers in chunks and discard seeds. Using metal blade, process garlic until chopped. Add onion and process with on-off bursts until coarsely chopped; combine with mushrooms. Process green peppers with on-off bursts until finely chopped; combine with mushroom-onion mixture. Add vegetable mixture to pan drippings and cook, stirring, over medium heat until onion is soft (about 5 minutes).

Process parsley until finely chopped. Add water, wine, tomato paste, salt, marjoram, oregano, thyme, and stock base to parsley and process for 3 seconds to blend. Pour onto cooked vegetables. (If you use a bouillon cube, do not place in food processor but add directly to cooked vegetables; cube is usually hard and may become wedged between processor bowl and blade.)

Return chicken (except breast pieces) to pan. Bring to a boil, reduce heat, cover, and simmer for

25 minutes. Add breast pieces and continue to simmer, covered, for about 20 more minutes, or until meat is no longer pink in thickest part (cut a small gash to test). Makes 4 or 5 servings.

Plum-glazed Chicken

Quickly made from canned plums, this sweet-tart sauce gives a colorful glaze to baked chicken. Another time you might prepare the sauce to baste a leg of lamb or roast pork during the last 45 minutes of cooking.

    1 medium-size onion
    2 tablespoons butter or margarine
    1 can (1 lb.) purple plums
    ⅓ cup firmly packed brown sugar
    ¼ cup tomato-based chili sauce
    2 tablespoons soy sauce
    1 teaspoon ground ginger
    2 teaspoons lemon juice
    3- pound broiler-fryer chicken, cut in
         pieces
       Salt and pepper

Cut onion in chunks. Using metal blade, process onion with on-off bursts until finely chopped. Heat butter in a wide frying pan; add onion and cook, stirring, over medium heat until limp (about 5 minutes). Meanwhile, remove pits from plums. Process plums and plum syrup until puréed. Add purée to onion along with brown sugar, chili sauce, soy sauce, ginger, and lemon juice. Cook, uncovered, over medium heat for 15 minutes or until slightly thickened, stirring frequently.

Sprinkle chicken with salt and pepper and arrange, skin side down, in a lightly greased baking pan. Bake in a 350° oven for 30 minutes, basting with sauce after each 15 minutes. Turn chicken skin side up and bake for another 30 minutes, basting with sauce several times. Chicken is done when meat is no longer pink in thickest part (cut a small gash to test). Heat remaining sauce and pass at table. Makes 4 or 5 servings.

Cream Puff Chicken

If you're looking for a party dish with flair, try boned chicken baked in a crisp overcoat of classic French pastry. You can make it a day ahead, then give it the final baking just minutes before serving.

Start with boned **chicken breasts** or boned **thighs** or a combination of the two. Plan on 1 or 2 pieces of chicken per serving. Sprinkle **chicken** lightly on all sides with **salt, pepper,** and crushed dry **rosemary.** Place chicken, skin side up, on a rack in a broiling pan and tuck chicken edges under so each piece makes a compact bundle 3 to 4 inches square. Broil

4 inches from heat until golden on 1 side (about 10 minutes). Remove from heat and let cool. Transfer pieces, skin side up, to a lightly greased baking pan, leaving 2 inches between pieces.

For the coating, prepare **chou paste** (See Cream Puffs, page 65). Spread ¼ to ⅓ cup chou paste (depending on the size of the pieces) evenly over each piece of chicken. Cover pan with foil (foil should not touch pastry) and refrigerate for at least 2 hours or until next day.

To cook, remove foil and bake chicken in a 425° oven for 35 minutes or until pastry is brown and puffed. Transfer chicken to a serving platter and serve at once.

Burmese Chicken Curry

This curry is subtly spiced. The onion and garlic in the sauce take on a surprising mildness as they cook.

    5 medium-size onions
    5 small, dried hot chile peppers, seeds
         removed
    1 tablespoon coarsely chopped fresh ginger
         root or 1½ teaspoons ground ginger
   10 cloves garlic
    1½ teaspoons salt
    ½ teaspoon turmeric
    3- pound broiler-fryer chicken, cut in
         pieces
    ¼ cup salad oil
    1 can (about 1 lb.) tomatoes
    ⅓ cup water
    1 tablespoon soy sauce
    1 teaspoon grated lemon peel

Cut 3 of the onions to fit feed tube; slice, using slicing disc. Set aside. Cut remaining 2 onions in chunks. Using metal blade, process the 2 onions, chile peppers, ginger, and garlic until puréed.

Mix together salt and turmeric; rub chicken with mixture. Heat oil in a wide frying pan over medium-high heat. Add chicken and cook, turning once, until it is browned (about 10 minutes). Remove chicken, then add sliced onion and puréed onion mixture to pan. Cook, stirring occasionally, until sliced onion is very limp.

Process tomatoes and their liquid until smooth; add to onions along with water, soy sauce, and lemon peel. Return chicken (except breast pieces) to pan. Cover and simmer for 25 minutes. Add breast pieces and continue to simmer, covered, for about 20 more minutes, or until meat is no longer pink in thickest part (cut a small gash to test).

With a slotted spoon, remove chicken pieces to a serving platter and keep warm. Boil sauce, uncovered, stirring constantly, until reduced to about 3 cups. Skim off fat and discard; spoon sauce over chicken. Makes 4 or 5 servings.

Turkey Bacon Logs

A crisp bacon wrapping flavors these juicy turkey patties; serve them for breakfast or dinner.

    2 cups (1 lb.) raw boned turkey meat (dark or
         light), cut in 1-inch chunks
    4 green onions
    ½ cup packed parsley sprigs
    1 egg
    ¼ cup fine dry bread crumbs
    ¼ teaspoon *each* salt, pepper, and poultry
         seasoning
    8 strips bacon

Using metal blade, process turkey, ⅓ at a time, with 3 long bursts, until finely chopped; set aside. Cut onions and ½ of tops into 1-inch lengths. Process with parsley until finely chopped. Add egg, bread crumbs, salt, pepper, and poultry seasoning and process for 2 seconds. Distribute turkey meat over parsley mixture and process for 2 more seconds to blend.

Divide mixture into 8 equal portions and shape each into a 2-inch-long log. Wrap each log with 1 strip bacon and secure ends with wooden picks. Place on rack in broiler pan. Bake in a 425° oven for 40 minutes or until bacon is brown and crisp. Makes 4 servings.

Turkey and Vegetable Tumble

Boned meat from turkey parts, chopped in the food processor, provides the basis for this delicious and economical entrée.

    1 carrot
    1 stalk celery
    1 small onion
    ¼ pound mushrooms
    1 can (8 oz.) water chestnuts, drained
    2 cups (1 lb.) raw boned turkey meat (dark or
         light), cut in 1-inch chunks
    4 tablespoons salad oil
    1 cup frozen peas, thawed
    ½ teaspoon salt
    1 tablespoon cornstarch
    3 tablespoons oyster sauce
    ⅔ cup regular-strength chicken broth
         About 40 butter lettuce or romaine leaves,
         washed and chilled

Cut carrot, celery, and onion in chunks. Using metal blade, process carrot, celery, onion, mushrooms, and water chestnuts separately with on-off bursts until coarsely chopped. Combine chopped vegetables in a bowl. Process turkey, 1 cup at a time, with three 2-second bursts or until coarsely chopped.

Heat 2 tablespoons of the oil in a wide frying pan over high heat. Add turkey and cook, stirring to break up meat, until it is no longer pink (3 to 4 minutes; if you use only white meat, cook 2 to 3 minutes). Turn out of pan.

Add remaining 2 tablespoons oil to pan. When oil is hot, add chopped vegetables and peas and cook, stirring, over high heat for 3 minutes.

Stir together salt, cornstarch, oyster sauce, and broth; add to pan. Add turkey and cook, stirring, until mixture thickens and boils (about 1 minute).

Pour meat mixture into a serving dish and accompany with a separate container of lettuce. To eat, spoon filling into a lettuce leaf and wrap leaf around it. Makes 4 main-dish servings.

Poultry Stuffing

There are many ways to vary this old-fashioned poultry stuffing. You can start with white or whole wheat bread or cornbread, then add a variety of options to suit your taste. This amount is sufficient for a large chicken or four Cornish game hens. Make three times the recipe for a 12 to 14-pound turkey.

         About 6 slices day-old bread
    1 teaspoon salt
    ¼ teaspoon pepper
    ½ teaspoon *each* marjoram and sage leaves
    1 small onion
    1 stalk celery
         Chicken or turkey giblets (optional)
    ⅓ cup butter or margarine
         About 1 tablespoon regular-strength
         chicken broth or milk

Leave bread out, uncovered, for a few hours to dry slightly. Tear slices in quarters and, using the metal blade, process 2 pieces at a time to make coarse crumbs; you should have 4 cups loosely packed crumbs. Transfer to a large bowl and toss with salt, pepper, marjoram, and sage.

Cut onion and celery in chunks. Process together with on-off bursts until coarsely chopped. If you use giblets, cut in half, then process separately until finely minced. Melt butter in a wide frying pan over medium heat. Add onion-celery mixture and giblets; stirring, cook until onion is limp and golden (about 5 minutes). Add to bread crumbs and toss lightly with a fork until ingredients are thoroughly mixed. Sprinkle broth over mixture, tossing with a fork *just* until barely moistened. Loosely stuff bird.

USE YOUR FOOD PROCESSOR to help you make a speedy and unusual picnic. Clockwise from upper left: sliced and whole raw vegetables and Crunchy Egg Dip (page 11), Picnic-style Chicken (page 44), and hot corn on the cob with Fines Herbes Butter (page 17).

Vegetables

If you want your food processor to be a real time saver, use it daily for preparing vegetables. It will quickly slice or shred your favorite fresh vegetables; then you can steam or butter-steam them in no time with a small piece of butter and a spoonful or two of water. In this chapter you will find suggestions to surprise your palate and vary your menu while enjoying the fresh, natural flavor of vegetables.

Tomato Pizza

(Pictured on front cover)

A quick, no-rising pizza base topped with fresh vegetables and cheese is an easy way to get rid of vegetable boredom. This is a good recipe for the first-time pizza maker; you mix the dough and prepare most of the toppings with the food processor. If you like an entrée to include meat, top with slices of salami or kielbasa.

  1 cup water
  2 tablespoons shortening
3¼ cups all-purpose flour, unsifted
  2 tablespoons sugar
  1 teaspoon salt
  1 package active dry yeast
  1 egg
  2 tablespoons olive oil or salad oil
  4 medium-size tomatoes
 ¼ pound mushrooms
  1 green pepper
  8 ounces provolone, mozzarella, or jack cheese
  1 small onion
     Tomato sauce (recipe follows)
  1 can (2¼ oz.) sliced ripe olives, drained
 ¼ cup grated Parmesan cheese
 ½ pound salami or kielbasa (optional)

In a small pan, heat water and shortening just until shortening melts; remove from heat and let stand until tepid (110°). Using metal blade, process 1½ cups of the flour, sugar, salt, and yeast for 2 seconds to mix. With motor running, pour shortening mixture slowly through the feed tube. Add egg and process for 2 seconds to mix. Sprinkle over another 1½ cups of the flour and process until dough forms a ball.

Sprinkle remaining ¼ cup flour on a board, turn dough onto it, and knead until smooth and elastic and most of flour has been absorbed (3 to 4 minutes). Divide dough in half. Pull and stretch each piece of dough to form a 12-inch circle, then transfer each piece onto a 12-inch greased pizza pan. (If time is not short, let dough rest for 30 minutes before shaping; this eliminates elasticity.) Rub 1 tablespoon of oil over each pan of dough and let stand in a warm place while you prepare topping.

With a knife, cut tomatoes into ¼-inch-thick slices; set aside. Using slicing disc, slice mushrooms and salami; set aside. Cut green pepper in half and discard seeds. Stand halves in feed tube and slice; set aside. Change to shredding disc and shred cheese; set aside. Change to metal blade. Cut onion in chunks and process with on-off bursts until coarsely chopped.

To assemble pizza, spread tomato sauce (recipe follows) over dough. Arrange slices of tomato, mushroom, salami, and green pepper over sauce. Sprinkle onion, olives, and cheeses over all.

Bake one pizza at a time on lowest rack of a 500° oven until crust is browned (7 to 10 minutes). Cut hot pizzas in wedges to serve. Makes 4 to 6 main-dish servings.

Tomato Sauce. Using metal blade, process 2 cloves **garlic** until chopped. Cut 1 large **onion** into chunks, add to garlic, and process with on-off bursts until finely chopped. Heat 2 tablespoons **salad oil** in a wide frying pan over medium-high heat, add onion mixture, and stirring occasionally, cook until golden (about 5 minutes). Remove pan from heat and stir in 2 cans (6 oz. *each*) **tomato paste,** 1 teaspoon **salt,** ½ teaspoon *each* **marjoram, thyme,** and **oregano** leaves, and ½ teaspoon dry **basil.** Makes enough sauce to cover 2 pizzas.

Vegetable Pie

Similar to a quiche but without a crust, this cheese and vegetable dish combines many flavors of a summer harvest. Serve it as an entrée with soup or salad, or serve it as a casserole with meat.

    8   ounces mozzarella cheese
    1   small zucchini
    3   large mushrooms
    1   clove garlic
    1   medium-size onion
    1   small eggplant (about 1 lb.)
    ¼   cup salad oil
    ¾   teaspoon *each* dry basil and oregano
          leaves
    ½   teaspoon salt
    ⅛   teaspoon pepper
    3   large tomatoes
    4   eggs
    ½   cup grated Parmesan cheese
          Paprika

Insert shredding disc in processor, shred mozzarella cheese and set aside. Change to slicing disc; slice zucchini and mushrooms and set aside. Change to metal blade. Process garlic until chopped. Cut onion into chunks, add to garlic, and process with on-off bursts until coarsely chopped; set aside. Peel eggplant and cut into chunks. Process ½ at a time with on-off bursts until very coarsely chopped.

Heat salad oil in a wide frying pan over medium heat. Add eggplant and onion; stirring occasionally, cook for 10 minutes or until vegetables are soft. Add zucchini, mushrooms, basil, oregano, salt, and pepper, and cook for 7 minutes or until mushrooms are soft.

Meanwhile, peel and quarter tomatoes. Process with on-off bursts until coarsely chopped. Add to eggplant mixture and simmer rapidly until all liquid has evaporated (about 15 minutes). Cool.

Process eggs and ¼ cup of the Parmesan cheese for 5 seconds to mix. Stir into cooled eggplant mixture. Pour half of this into a well greased 9-inch pie

(Continued on next page)

Vegetable Toppings

Chopped parsley is one of the simplest and best garnishes for vegetables. Process a bunch at a time and keep it in a jar in the refrigerator for instant use. Here are three other ways to complement freshly cooked vegetables.

Savory Cheese Sauce

There are many ways to use this low-calorie topping—try it on baked or boiled potatoes or over carrots, green beans, or Brussels sprouts.

Using metal blade, process ¼ cup packed **parsley sprigs** until finely chopped. Add a ¼-inch-thick slice of medium-size **onion** and process until chopped. Add 1 cup **cottage cheese,** 1 tablespoon **lemon juice,** ½ cup unflavored **yogurt,** 1 teaspoon **sugar,** ¼ teaspoon *each* **salt** and **dill weed,** and a dash of **pepper.** Process until mixture is smooth. Makes about 1½ cups.

Buttered Crumb Topping

This topping gives a finished look to broccoli, cauliflower, asparagus, or green beans.

Break 4 slices of **crisp dry bread** into quarters. Using metal blade, process to make fine crumbs; you should have 1 cup. Melt ¼ cup **butter** or margarine in a wide frying pan over medium heat. Add crumbs and, stirring occasionally, cook until browned (about 5 minutes); let cool.

Meanwhile, process ¼ cup packed **parsley sprigs** until finely chopped. Cut 2 **hard-cooked eggs** into quarters, add to parsley, and process with on-off bursts until finely chopped. Combine with crumbs and sprinkle over hot cooked vegetables. Makes about 1¼ cups.

Hollandaise Sauce

Serve this classic sauce over asparagus, green beans, broccoli, or cabbage wedges; or use it as a dipping sauce for artichokes.

Using plastic or metal blade, process 3 **egg yolks** (at room temperature) and 1½ tablespoons **lemon juice** for 2 seconds to mix. Melt ¾ cup **butter** or margarine just until it bubbles. Add 1 tablespoon **hot water** to egg mixture and process for 2 seconds. With motor still running, pour hot butter through feed tube in a slow steady stream. Turn off motor. Add ½ teaspoon **salt,** 1 teaspoon **Dijon mustard,** and a dash of **cayenne;** process for 2 seconds.

Serve at once. Of, if sauce is to be used within several hours, leave at room temperature, then reheat over hot but not boiling water; stir until smooth. Freeze any leftover hollandaise in a small jar. To serve, thaw at room temperature and reheat as directed above. Makes about 1½ cups.

. . . *Vegetable Pie (cont'd.)*

pan (1¼ inches deep) or 8-inch square baking pan. Top with half the mozzarella cheese, then top with remaining vegetable mixture. Sprinkle with remaining cheeses, then lightly with paprika.

Bake in a 400° oven for 25 minutes or until puffed and browned. Cool on rack for 10 minutes, then cut in wedges or spoon out portions. Makes 4 to 6 servings.

Savory Summer Squash

When having guests for dinner, you can shred the squash and combine it with seasonings ahead of time.

- 2 pounds zucchini, crookneck, or patty pan squash
- ¼ cup butter or margarine
- 2 tablespoons water
- ½ teaspoon *each* salt and dry basil
- ⅛ teaspoon *each* pepper and garlic powder
- 1 cup sour cream
- 1 tablespoon all-purpose flour

Insert shredding disc in food processor. Cut squash in pieces to fit the feed tube; shred. In a wide frying pan, combine butter, water, salt, basil, pepper, and garlic powder. Mix in squash. Cover and cook over medium heat until squash is just tender (about 5 minutes). Remove cover for the last minute or two to evaporate most of the liquid.

Meanwhile, mix sour cream with flour until smooth; stir into squash. Bring to a boil, stirring until blended into a smooth sauce. Makes 6 to 8 servings.

Creamy Cabbage

Cream cheese provides a quick sauce for crisp-tender cabbage. For variety you could use cream cheese flavored with pimento rather than chives.

- 1 medium-size head (1½ to 2 lbs.) cabbage
- 2 tablespoons butter or margarine
- 1 small package (3 oz.) cream cheese with chives
- 1 teaspoon salt
- ¼ teaspoon pepper

Cut cabbage in wedges to fit feed tube; discard core. Slice, using slicing disc. Melt butter in a wide frying pan over medium-high heat. Add cabbage, cover, and cook until crisp-tender (about 5 minutes).

Meanwhile, cut cream cheese in small cubes. Distribute over cabbage and stir lightly until it melts into pan juices. Season with salt and pepper. Makes 6 servings.

Creamed Spinach

All the fresh flavor and bright color of raw spinach are retained in this dish because the spinach is only heated through and not cooked. Other greens, such as Swiss chard or beet greens, may be presented this way, too.

- 1 pound fresh spinach
- 4 slices bacon, crisp-fried and drained (optional)
- 2 tablespoons butter or margarine
- 2 tablespoons all-purpose flour
- 1 cup half-and-half (light cream)
- ½ teaspoon *each* salt and Worcestershire Dash *each* of dry mustard and pepper

Wash spinach, pat dry with paper towels, and discard heavy stems. Cut spinach leaves crosswise in thirds. Using metal blade, process spinach, ⅓ at a time, with on-off bursts until finely chopped; set aside. Process bacon until coarsely chopped.

Melt butter in a wide frying pan over medium heat. Add flour and, stirring, cook for 2 minutes or until flour is golden. Pour in half-and-half and, stirring, cook until sauce is smooth and thick. Season with salt, Worcestershire, mustard, and pepper. Add chopped, uncooked spinach and bring just to boiling. Stir in bacon just before serving. Makes 4 servings.

Duxelles

In French cooking, a dry mushroom mixture called *duxelles* is frequently used to give an intensified mushroom flavor to meat, fish, or poultry. It also makes an elegant addition to stuffings, mushroom sauce, scrambled eggs, omelets, and vegetable dishes. For convenience, you might prepare several batches of duxelles and freeze them in ½-cup portions.

- 1 pound mushrooms
- 2 shallots or the white part only of 2 green onions
- ¼ cup butter or margarine
  Salt and pepper

Rinse and drain mushrooms; break in quarters if large. Using metal blade, process mushrooms, ½ at a time, with on-off bursts until very finely chopped but not puréed. Transfer to a bowl. Process shallots with on-off bursts until finely chopped.

Turn mushrooms, a handful at a time, into a clean dish towel and twist towel over a bowl to squeeze out all liquid. (Save liquid for sauce or soup.)

Melt butter in a wide frying pan over medium-high heat. Crumble mushrooms into pan, add shallots, and cook, stirring frequently, until liquid evaporates and mixture is dark brown (about 8 minutes). Add salt and pepper to taste. Spoon into small containers, cover, and refrigerate for 1 week or freeze for longer storage. Makes 1 cup.

Deviled Green Beans

This flavorful dish is a perfect accompaniment to barbecued or roasted meat.

    4 ounces Cheddar cheese
    1 clove garlic
    1 medium-size onion
    ½ green pepper
    1 jar (2 oz.) sliced pimentos, drained
    2 tablespoons butter or margarine
    2 teaspoons prepared mustard
    1 can (8 oz.) tomato sauce
    ½ teaspoon salt
    ¼ teaspoon pepper
    1 package (9 oz.) frozen cut green beans,
         cooked and drained

Insert shredding disc; shred cheese and set aside. Change to metal blade. Process garlic until chopped. Cut onion and green pepper into chunks; discard green pepper seeds. Add onion and green pepper to garlic and process with on-off bursts until coarsely chopped. Add pimentos and process with 2 on-off bursts.

Melt butter in a wide frying pan over medium-high heat. Add chopped vegetables and, stirring occasionally, cook until onion is limp (about 5 minutes). Remove from heat and stir in mustard, tomato sauce, salt, pepper, and beans. Turn into a 1-quart casserole; sprinkle cheese over the top. Bake in a 350° oven for 25 minutes or until cheese is melted. Makes 4 servings.

Barbecue-style Beans

(Pictured on page 39)

You can heat this bean dish over low coals if you serve it with barbecued meat, or simply warm it in the oven, if you prefer.

    1 clove garlic
    1 medium-size onion
    2 tablespoons salad oil
    ¼ cup packed parsley sprigs
    1 can (8 oz.) tomato sauce
    1 tablespoon chili powder
    ¼ teaspoon ground cumin
    ½ teaspoon salt
    3 cans (15 oz. *each*) pinto beans

Using metal blade, process garlic until chopped. Cut onion into chunks, add to garlic, and process

with on-off bursts until coarsely chopped. Heat oil in a wide frying pan over medium heat. Add onion and garlic and cook, stirring occasionally, until golden (about 5 minutes). Remove from heat. Process parsley until finely chopped. Add to onion along with tomato sauce, chili powder, cumin, and salt. Drain beans, saving ½ cup of the liquid. Add beans and liquid to pan and mix in thoroughly; then spoon into a 1½-quart casserole or a container which you can place on the grill. Bake in a 350° oven for 30 minutes or heat over low coals until hot. Makes 6 to 8 servings.

Crusty Potato Casserole

A cross between scalloped and mashed potatoes, this casserole is a good choice for brunch. You could easily double the recipe, too, for a dinner buffet.

    3 medium-size potatoes (about 1½ lbs.)
         Water
    1 large onion
    ½ cup milk
    2 tablespoons butter or margarine
    2 eggs
    1 teaspoon salt
    ¼ teaspoon pepper
         Paprika

Insert shredding disc; peel potatoes and shred; you should have 4 cups. Transfer potatoes to a bowl and cover with water to prevent discoloration. Change to metal blade. Cut onion into chunks and process with on-off bursts until coarsely chopped.

Remove ½ cup water from potatoes and place in a small pan with milk and 1 tablespoon of the butter; cook over medium heat to just under boiling; remove from heat. Process eggs, salt, and pepper for 3 seconds. With motor running, pour hot milk mixture slowly through the feed tube.

Drain potatoes well by pouring into a colander and pressing out the liquid. Combine potatoes, onion, and egg mixture. Rub the remaining 1 tablespoon butter over the sides and bottom of an 8-inch square baking pan. Spoon potato mixture into pan and sprinkle with paprika. Bake, uncovered, in a 375° oven until set in center and edges are browned and crusty (about 50 minutes). Cut in squares to serve. Makes 6 servings.

Potato Chips

(Pictured on page 31)

Making potato chips is like making popcorn — it's fun to do, and it's fun to eat them right out of the pan. You can fry the chips ahead and keep them crisp in a tightly covered container, but they taste best when eaten shortly after cooking.

(Continued on next page)

. . . *Potato Chips (cont'd.)*

To make the potato chips, use mature potatoes which are relatively high in starch, such as Russets or other kinds of baking potatoes. Choose small potatoes that will stand in the feed tube, or cut fat ones in half lengthwise to fit feed tube.

Scrub **potatoes** and leave the skins on for a natural chip, or peel if you want to be fancy. Slice potatoes, using slicing disc. (Although it is not essential, if you soak the potato slices in cold water for an hour before frying, they will brown more evenly because some starch will have been removed.)

In a heavy kettle or deep fat fryer, heat 2 inches of **salad oil** to 340°. If potato slices are very thin, heat oil only to 320°. Add slices (pat dry first if soaked in water), a handful at a time, and cook until crisp and lightly browned (about 1½ to 2 minutes). Remove with a slotted spoon and drain on paper towels. Season lightly with **salt,** seasoning salt, or garlic salt, and munch.

Hot Fried Potato Chips. Scrub 4 unpeeled baking **potatoes;** cut in pieces to fit feed tube. Slice potatoes, using slicing disc. Slice 2 small **onions** and separate rings. Melt 3 tablespoons **butter** or margarine in a wide frying pan over medium heat. Add potatoes, a few at a time, and coat each slice well with butter, turning frequently and adding more butter (1 to 2 tablespoons at a time) as needed to keep potatoes from sticking. Push potatoes to sides of pan; add onion and **salt** and **pepper** to taste. Cook, turning over often, until vegetables are golden brown. Cover pan and cook until potatoes are tender (about 5 minutes). Makes 4 servings.

Slow-cooked Onions

(Pictured on page 31)

Slow and gentle cooking changes the rather harsh flavor of raw onions to a mellow, rich sweetness. Serve them on beef patties or broiled steak, simply prepared poultry or fish, or with other vegetables such as green beans, peas, or carrots.

6 **medium-size onions**
3 **tablespoons butter or margarine**

Insert slicing disc in food processor. Cut onions in half lengthwise. Stand them in feed tube and slice; then separate slices. Melt butter in a wide frying pan. Add onion and cook, uncovered, over medium heat for about 30 minutes, stirring occasionally at first and more frequently as slices begin to develop a golden color. The onions should not show signs of browning for at least 15 minutes — if they do, reduce heat.

When onions are generally a light gold and a few bits are browned, remove from heat. Serve onions hot; or chill, covered, for 3 or 4 days. To reheat, place desired quantity in a small pan and heat, stirring. Makes 4 to 5 servings.

Chinese Stir-fried Vegetables

(Pictured on facing page)

Nothing takes the place of a knife when it comes to cutting the intricate vegetable shapes often called for in Chinese cooking. But the rules for cutting are not rigid, and many vegetables can be sliced for stir-frying with a food processor. These include green or red bell peppers, onions, carrots, turnips, celery, mushrooms, and all varieties of summer squash.

The following recipe provides a basic guideline for stir-fried vegetables. You can combine two or three vegetables to suit your taste. For a real Chinese flavor, undercook the vegetables slightly so they will still be crisp and bright.

1 **to 1½ pounds vegetables (suggestions below)**
¼ **cup water**
1½ **teaspoons cornstarch**
1 **teaspoon soy sauce**
2 **tablespoons salad oil**
2 **slices fresh ginger root**
½ **teaspoon salt**
1 **to 2 tablespoons water**
¼ **cup cashew nuts (optional)**
    Coriander (cilantro), often called Chinese parsley, for garnish

Use a single vegetable or combine several vegetables which complement each other. Green pepper, onion, and zucchini combine well; so do carrots, celery, and onion. Cut vegetables in pieces that will stand in feed tube. Slice, using slicing disc, and discard any end pieces that were not evenly sliced. Mix the ¼ cup water, cornstarch, and soy sauce in a small bowl. Assemble remaining ingredients for ready use while cooking.

Heat wok or wide frying pan over high heat. Add oil, heat, and swirl around wok. Add ginger and cook for 15 seconds to release flavor; remove ginger and discard.

Add vegetables and salt, and cook and stir for 30 seconds to coat vegetables with oil. Add the 1 tablespoon water, cover, and cook over high heat until vegetables are crisp-tender (1½ to 2 minutes). If you cook firm vegetables such as carrots, add an extra tablespoon of water if wok appears dry.

Remove cover and stir in nuts if you wish. Stir cornstarch mixture again to blend it, pour into wok, and stir and cook until sauce thickens (about 30 seconds). Garnish with sprigs of coriander. Makes 4 to 6 servings.

FAST SLICING with a food processor and flash cooking in a wok add up to a super-quick way to prepare Chinese Stir-fried Vegetables (recipe above).

Pasta, Eggs, & Cheese

The food processor is a natural for preparing pasta dishes. There are vegetables to slice and chop for sauce, and chunks of cheese to shred. Parmesan cheese, freshly grated, turns the simplest noodle or spaghetti dish into very special food. And if you feel adventuresome and want to try something that is fun and flavor-rewarding, make your own velvety egg noodles at home. The project is not difficult and the food processor cuts in half the time it takes to mix and knead the dough. This chapter also explores some delicious ways to combine eggs and cheese for brunch or light entrées.

Fresh Egg Noodles

(Pictured on pages 56-57)

Making a batch of egg noodles by hand for a family meal or a first course for guests is not a big job. If you use a pasta machine you can prepare enough for a crowd and let your guests share in the fun.

    1¾ cups all-purpose flour, unsifted
     1 teaspoon olive oil or salad oil
     ½ teaspoon salt
     2 large eggs
     2 tablespoons water

Using metal blade, process flour, oil, salt, and eggs for 5 seconds or until mixture looks like cornmeal. With motor running, pour water slowly down feed tube and process until dough forms a ball. Dough should be well blended but not sticky. If it feels sticky, cut dough in 3 pieces, sprinkle in another tablespoon of flour, and process again to form a ball. If dough looks crumbly (this may happen if you use flour which has been in your cupboard a long time), add another teaspoon or two of water to form dough. If food processor begins to slow down or stop (a good indication that dough is properly mixed), turn off motor and proceed to next step.

Turn dough onto a floured board and knead until it is very smooth and elastic—mixing action of food processor reduces kneading time from 10 minutes to 2 or 3. (If you will be using a pasta machine later, it is not necessary to knead dough at all, as squeezing action of machine is equivalent of kneading.) Slip dough into a plastic bag and let rest for 30 minutes. Then shape noodles by hand or use pasta machine.

To shape noodles by hand. On a floured board, divide dough into 4 equal portions. Roll out 1 portion at a time into a rectangle about 8 inches wide and 10 to 12 inches long—it will be ¹/₁₆ inch thick. Transfer to lightly floured sheets of wax paper and let sit uncovered while you roll out rest of dough (this drying will prevent dough from sticking together later).

Starting at a narrow end, roll up each strip of dough jelly-roll fashion and cut in ¼-inch-wide strips. Pick up each end of dough and unfurl the coil as you might a paper serpentine. Cook at once, or let dry for another 30 minutes, place in plastic bag, and refrigerate for as long as 2 days. Makes about 12 ounces fresh noodles.

To shape noodles with a pasta machine. Divide dough into 3 equal portions. Working with 1 portion at a time, feed dough through machine's smooth rollers, set as far apart as possible. Fold dough into thirds and repeat feeding process 8 to 10 times (this is actually kneading). Whenever dough appears moist or sticky, lightly flour it and sprinkle flour on rollers.

Set rollers closer together and feed dough through again. Cut length of dough in half if necessary for easier handling. Keep repeating feeding process, setting rollers closer together each time, until dough goes through the finest or next-to-finest setting. Dough will double and triple in length as it becomes thinner, so cut it in half, crosswise, whenever necessary for easier handling.

Cut final strip into 10 to 12-inch lengths. Then feed dough through blades of cutting section — it helps to have another person catch noodles as they emerge from machine. Cook at once, or let dry for 30 minutes, place in a plastic bag, and refrigerate for as long as 2 days. Makes about 12 ounces fresh noodles.

To cook noodles. Fill a 6-quart kettle with at least 4 quarts **water.** Add 1 teaspoon **salt** and 1 tablespoon **salad oil;** bring to a boil. Drop **noodles** into rapidly boiling water. Return to boiling and cook, uncovered, on high heat for about 2 to 3 minutes or until *al dente* (tender to bite). Drain in colander. To serve, toss with 6 to 8 tablespoons melted **butter** and freshly grated **Parmesan cheese** (page 58), or top with sauce of your choice. Makes about 4 cups cooked noodles or 3 to 4 main-dish servings.

Whole Wheat Egg Noodles

For an interesting change, you can make noodles with whole wheat flour. They have a chewy yet tender texture and a healthy whole grain flavor.

Using metal blade, process 1¼ cups stoneground **whole wheat flour** (unsifted), ¼ cup **wheat germ,** ¾ teaspoon **salt,** 1 teaspoon **olive oil** or salad oil, and 2 large **eggs** for 5 seconds or until mixture looks like cornmeal. With motor running, add 1 tablespoon **water** through feed tube and process until dough forms a ball.

To knead and roll dough and to cut and cook noodles, follow directions for fresh egg noodles (preceding). Cook as directed, increasing cooking time to 5 to 7 minutes. Drain and toss with 2 to 4 tablespoons **butter** or margarine and ½ to 1 cup grated **Parmesan cheese** (page 58). Makes 4 cups cooked noodles or 6 to 8 side-dish servings.

Carbonara Sauce

Richly flavored Italian sausage and prosciutto flavor this sauce for spaghetti.

    1   cup packed parsley sprigs
    ¼   pound mild Italian pork sausage
    ¼   pound prosciutto or cooked ham
    2   tablespoons butter or margarine
    3   eggs
    ½   cup freshly grated Parmesan, Romano, or
           asiago cheese (page 58)
        Freshly ground black pepper
    4   cups hot cooked, drained spaghetti

Using metal blade, process parsley until finely chopped; set aside. Remove casing from sausage; cut sausage and prosciutto in chunks. Process meats together with long on-off bursts until finely chopped. Heat butter in a wide frying pan over medium-low heat. Add meat and, stirring occasionally, cook until sausage is lightly browned

(about 10 minutes). Remove from heat.

Wash processor bowl and blade and reassemble. Process eggs, cheese, and a dash of pepper for 30 seconds. To meat, add spaghetti, egg mixture, and parsley; mix lightly. Makes 4 main-dish or 8 first-course servings.

Sauce Julio

(Pictured on page 57)

This very basic, quickly made tomato sauce is good with many kinds of pasta.

    3   tablespoons olive oil or salad oil
    2   cloves garlic
    1   small carrot
    1   cup packed parsley sprigs
    2   tablespoons fresh basil leaves or
           2 teaspoons dry basil
    1   teaspoon oregano leaves
    ½   pound mushrooms
    2   cans (8 oz. *each*) tomato sauce
    1   can (10½ oz.) regular-strength beef broth
    ½   teaspoon salt
    ¼   teaspoon pepper
    4   to 5 cups hot, cooked, drained spaghetti,
           noodles, tortellini, or ravioli
        Freshly grated Parmesan cheese (page 58)

Place oil in a wide frying pan. Using metal blade, process garlic until chopped. Cut carrot in chunks, add to garlic, and process until finely chopped. Transfer to pan. Process parsley, basil, and oregano until parsley is finely chopped; add to pan. Using slicing disc, slice mushrooms; add to pan.

Stirring occasionally, cook vegetables over medium-high heat for 5 minutes, or until limp. Add tomato sauce, beef broth, salt, and pepper. Reduce heat to low, and simmer, uncovered, for 30 minutes. Mix sauce with pasta, sprinkle with Parmesan, and serve. Makes about 3 cups sauce; on pasta, makes 4 to 6 first-course servings.

Pesto Sauce

Pesto, one of the great Italian sauces, is relatively mild and very easy to like. The main ingredient, fresh basil (sweet basil or basilico) is a popular garden herb, available from spring through fall. If you don't grow your own, buy it from the produce section of your favorite market.

    2   cups packed fresh basil leaves, washed and
           drained well
    1   cup freshly grated Parmesan cheese (page 58)
    ½   cup olive oil

Using metal blade, process basil, cheese, and oil until basil is finely chopped (about 30 seconds). Use

(Continued on page 58)

Pasta, Eggs, & Cheese **55**

CLASSIC INGREDIENTS, so pure and simple that they could grace an artist's canvas, are the components of Fresh Egg Noodles (page 54).

PASTA MACHINE *eases process of rolling and cutting Fresh Egg Noodles. You can roll dough and shape noodles by hand, too.*

FRESH CARROTS AND BASIL *enhance tomato sauce in versatile Sauce Julio (page 55), pièce de résistance for Fresh Egg Noodles.*

at once; or place in small jars, cover surface with a thin layer of olive oil to prevent darkening, and refrigerate up to a week, or freeze for longer storage. Makes about 1⅓ cups.

Pasta with Pesto. To 4 cups hot cooked, drained flat **noodles,** spaghetti, or similar pasta, add 6 tablespoons **pesto sauce** and 4 tablespoons **butter** or margarine, at room temperature; mix quickly with two forks. Add 1 cup freshly grated **Parmesan cheese** (directions below) and mix. Serve with more cheese and pesto, to be added to taste. Makes 4 to 6 first-course servings.

Chile-Egg Puff

Good for brunch or a light supper, this quick-to-make baked egg dish has a mild Mexican flavor.

        8   ounces jack cheese
        5   eggs
        1   cup cottage cheese
        ¼   cup butter or margarine, melted and cooled
        ¼   cup all-purpose flour, unsifted
        ½   teaspoon baking powder
        ¼   teaspoon salt
        1   can (4 oz.) diced California green chiles

How to Process Hard Cheese

All forms of pasta have a special affinity for cheese. Parmesan is called for most frequently in the recipes in this chapter. Two other hard cheeses — Romano and asiago — are widely available, and they can be used interchangeably with Parmesan. All three are superb when freshly grated.

To grate any hard cheese with a food processor, cut away the tough, hard edges of the cheese. This part has very little flavor, so you can discard it. Or, if you prefer, cut it in slivers with a knife and add to Italian-style soup a few minutes before serving — depending on the dryness of the cheese, the slivers may only partially melt. Cut the cheese in 1-inch cubes. Fit the metal blade in the food processor, turn the motor on, and drop the cheese, a few pieces at a time, down the feed tube. Continue until all the cheese is processed (grated). For convenient storage, transfer the cheese to glass jars, cover, and store in the refrigerator for a week, or freeze for longer storage.

Insert shredding disc, shred jack cheese, and set aside. Change to plastic or metal blade. Process eggs for 10 seconds. Add cottage cheese and butter and process for 10 seconds. Add flour, baking powder, and salt and process with 2 on-off bursts. Add shredded cheese and chiles and process for only 1 second or just until blended.

Pour into a greased 8-inch-square baking pan. Bake in a 350° oven for 35 minutes or until edges are lightly browned and center appears firm. Makes 6 to 8 servings.

If you wish to serve this as an appetizer instead of a main dish, spoon 1½ tablespoons of mixture into 1½-inch muffin pans. Bake for 15 to 18 minutes or until firm. Makes 40 appetizers.

Omelet for Two

(Pictured on page 60)

Prepare one large omelet, then cut it in half to serve two, so you can sit down to a leisurely breakfast and savor the goodness while it is piping hot.

        1   small onion
        3   tablespoons butter or margarine
        4   large or 8 medium-size mushrooms
        2   ounces jack cheese
        ¼   cup packed parsley sprigs
        4   eggs
        1   tablespoon water
        ¼   teaspoon salt
            Dash of pepper

Insert slicing disc and slice onion. Heat 1 tablespoon of the butter in a frying pan over medium-low heat. Add onion and, stirring occasionally, cook until limp but not browned (about 10 minutes); set aside. Slice mushrooms and cook in another tablespoon of the butter over medium-high heat until liquid evaporates (about 4 minutes); set aside. Change to shredding disc, shred cheese and reserve. Change to metal blade, chop parsley, and reserve. Rinse processor bowl and blade and reassemble. Process together eggs, water, salt, and pepper for 5 seconds.

Heat remaining 1 tablespoon butter until bubbly in an 8-inch omelet pan or frying pan on medium-high heat. Add egg mixture.

As soon as bottom of omelet begins to set, slip a spatula under edges and let uncooked egg flow into center of pan. Don't worry about appearance; the liquid egg will fill in any small holes. Omelet is done when egg no longer runs freely but top still looks liquid and creamy.

Arrange cooked onion in a strip across middle of omelet, then cover with a strip of cooked mushrooms. Sprinkle cheese, then parsley over all. Fold omelet in half, over filling, and turn out onto serving dish. Cut in half, crosswise, to serve. Makes 2 servings.

Huevos Rancheros (Ranch-style Eggs)

You might pair these eggs, cooked in a zesty tomato sauce, with cornsticks or warmed tortillas. Either way, they're good to serve for brunch or as a light supper entree.

- 2 ounces jack cheese
- 1 clove garlic
- 1 small onion
- ½ green pepper, seeded
- 2 tablespoons salad oil
- 1 can (about 1 lb.) tomatoes
- ½ teaspoon salt
- ½ to 1 teaspoon chili powder
- 1½ teaspoons all-purpose flour
- 6 eggs

Insert shredding disc, shred cheese, and set aside. Change to metal blade and process garlic until chopped. Cut onion and green pepper in chunks, add to garlic, and process with on-off bursts until coarsely chopped.

Heat oil in a wide frying pan over medium-high heat. Add vegetables and, stirring occasionally, cook until limp (about 4 minutes). Meanwhile, process together tomatoes and their liquid, salt, and chili powder with on-off bursts until tomatoes are coarsely chopped. Sprinkle flour over onion mixture and stir in. Add tomatoes and, stirring occasionally, cook over medium heat for 4 minutes or until sauce is thickened. (At this point you can cover and refrigerate until next day. Before adding eggs, reheat sauce over medium heat.)

With back of spoon, make 6 evenly spaced depressions in sauce. Break 1 egg into each depression. Sprinkle cheese over eggs. Cover pan and cook over low heat until eggs are done to your liking (7 to 10 minutes). Makes 3 to 6 servings.

Zucchini Frittata

Frittata is an Italian-style omelet made with eggs, vegetables, and cheese. Cut it in individual portions and eat it hot or cool for lunch, supper, or delicious picnic fare.

- 1 clove garlic
- 1 small onion
- 1 medium-size zucchini
- 2 large leaves Swiss chard
- 2 tablespoons salad oil
- 6 eggs
- ½ teaspoon salt
- ⅛ teaspoon pepper
- 1 cup freshly grated Parmesan cheese (page 58)

Using metal blade, process garlic until chopped. Cut onion and zucchini in chunks. Cut Swiss chard stems in 2-inch lengths; cut leaves in 2-inch-wide strips. Add onion, zucchini, and Swiss chard stems to garlic and process with on-off bursts until coarsely chopped. Set aside. Process leaves with 3 long bursts or until coarsely chopped.

Heat oil in wide frying pan over medium-high heat, add chopped vegetables, and, stirring occasionally, cook for 5 minutes or until vegetables are slightly limp. Remove from heat and cool slightly.

Process eggs, salt, and pepper for 3 seconds. Add cheese and vegetables and process with 2 on-off bursts to mix. Pour into a greased 9-inch-square baking pan. Bake in a 350° oven for 30 minutes or until lightly browned. Makes 9 servings.

Rolled Meat Crêpes

This dish is similar in flavor to cannelloni, but far less complicated to prepare. Tender crêpes, enclosing a meat and spinach filling, bubble under tomato sauce. The meat crêpes can be prepared in stages—both the crêpes and the filling can be made several days in advance.

- 12 to 16 crêpes (recipe follows)
- 1 clove garlic
- 1 small onion
- 1 tablespoon salad oil
- ½ pound lean ground beef
- ¼ pound bulk pork sausage or spicy pork breakfast sausage (page 36)
- 1 package (10 or 12 oz.) frozen chopped spinach, thawed
- ½ teaspoon *each* salt and oregano leaves
- ¼ teaspoon pepper
- 2 cans (8 oz. *each*) tomato sauce
- 8 ounces jack cheese

Prepare crêpes, or bring to room temperature if refrigerated. Using metal blade, process garlic until chopped. Cut onion in chunks, add to garlic, and process with on-off bursts until finely chopped. Heat oil in a wide frying pan over medium-high heat, add onion and garlic, and, stirring, cook until onion is soft but not browned (about 4 minutes). Add beef and sausage and cook, stirring occasionally, until meat is browned and crumbly. Pour off excess fat.

Squeeze spinach to eliminate water; distribute spinach over meat. Add salt, oregano, and pepper and cook over medium-high heat for 3 minutes or until all liquid has evaporated.

Process meat-spinach mixture with 3 on-off bursts to finely chop. Spoon ¼ cup of meat filling down center of each crêpe and roll to enclose. Set filled crêpes, side by side, seam side down, in a 9 x 13-inch baking dish. (At this point you can cover and refrigerate for as long as 3 days or freeze for longer storage.)

To serve, pour tomato sauce over crêpes. Shred cheese, using the shredding disc; sprinkle evenly

(Continued on page 61)

over tomato sauce. Bake in a 350° oven for 30 minutes (40 to 45 minutes if frozen) or until hot and bubbly. Makes 6 to 8 servings.

Crêpes. Using plastic or metal blade, process 1 cup **milk** and 3 **eggs** for 2 seconds. Add ⅔ cup unsifted **all-purpose flour,** then process for 5 seconds or until smooth. You can cook immediately, but crêpes will be more tender if batter stands for 1 hour.

Place a 6 or 7-inch crêpe pan (or other flat-bottomed frying pan of this size) on medium heat. When pan is hot, add ¼ teaspoon **butter** or margarine and swirl to coat surface. At once, pour in 1½ to 2 tablespoons batter, quickly tilting pan so batter flows over entire flat surface. (Don't worry if there are a few little holes.) Cook until surface appears dry and edge is lightly browned. With a spatula, turn and brown other side. Turn out of pan onto a plate. Repeat procedure for each crêpe, stacking them on plate.

If you do not plan to use cooked crêpes within a few hours, allow them to cool, package airtight, and refrigerate for as long as 4 days. Let crêpes come to room temperature before filling; they tear if cold. Makes 12 to 16 crêpes.

Quiche Lorraine

The trick to keeping the crust from becoming soggy is to prebake the pastry shell before pouring in the cheese-custard filling.

Pastry for a single-crust 9-inch pie or rich
    pie pastry (page 67)
 6 ounces Swiss cheese
10 strips bacon, crisp-fried and drained
 4 eggs
1¼ cups whipping cream
 ½ cup milk
    Freshly grated (or ground) nutmeg

Roll out pastry on lightly floured board to about ⅛-inch thickness. Fit into a 9-inch pie pan; crimp edges. Place a circle of foil inside pastry shell and partially fill with dry rice or beans. Bake in 350° oven for 20 minutes. Lift off rice and foil and return pastry to oven for 5 minutes. Let cool.

Using shredding disc, shred cheese; distribute over baked pastry shell. Change to metal blade and process bacon until chopped; sprinkle over cheese. Process eggs, cream, and milk for 5 seconds; pour over bacon. Sprinkle nutmeg over filling (about ⅛ teaspoon).

AFTER SLICING, CHOPPING, shredding, and kneading are all accomplished by your machine, Omelet for Two (page 58) and Quick Butter Croissants (page 71) are easy to make for breakfast.

Bake in a 325° oven for about 50 minutes or until a knife inserted in center comes out clean. Let stand for 10 minutes before cutting. Makes 6 servings.

Picnic Sausage Quiches

These are meaty, firm quiches. Baked individually in small foil tart pans, they are ideal to serve—warm or cool—at a picnic, to eat right out of the pan.

Pastry for a double-crust 9-inch pie or rich
    pie pastry (page 67)
 4 ounces Swiss cheese
 1 pound Polish sausage (kielbasa)
 ¼ pound mushrooms
 1 medium-size onion
 ½ small green pepper, seeded
 ½ cup packed parsley sprigs
 2 eggs
 ½ cup milk
 1 tablespoon Dijon mustard
 2 tablespoons grated Parmesan cheese

Divide pastry into 6 equal parts. To roll out pastry, follow directions for quiche Lorraine (preceding). Fit pastry into each of six 5-inch tart pans, and crimp edges. Set small circles of foil inside tart shells and partially fill with dry beans or rice. Bake in a 350° oven for 20 minutes. Lift off foil and beans and bake about 5 minutes longer or until lightly browned. Let cool.

To prepare filling, shred Swiss cheese with shredding disc; set cheese aside. Change to slicing disc. Remove casing from sausage and cut sausage in 3-inch lengths. Stand sausage snugly in feed tube and slice. Reserve 18 slices for garnish. Change to metal blade and process remaining sausage slices until finely chopped. Put chopped sausage into a wide frying pan and cook over medium heat until fat is released (about 2 to 3 minutes). Remove pan from heat; drain fat.

Process mushrooms with on-off bursts until finely chopped; add to sausage. Cut onion and green pepper in chunks; process with on-off bursts until finely chopped, then add to sausage. Return pan to medium heat and, stirring, cook until onion is soft but not browned (about 5 minutes). Remove pan from heat. Process parsley until finely chopped and stir into sausage mixture.

Process eggs, milk, and mustard for 3 seconds. Add to sausage mixture along with shredded Swiss cheese; mix to blend. Divide mixture equally among 6 prebaked pastry shells. Sprinkle reserved sausage slices and Parmesan cheese on each.

Bake filled tarts in 350° oven for 30 minutes or until a knife inserted in center comes out clean. Serve warm, or let cool, wrap well, and refrigerate for as long as 24 hours. Take out of refrigerator an hour before serving. Makes 6 tart-size quiches.

Desserts

It is exciting to prepare desserts with a food processor. When you learn the techniques of mixing and blending, you'll discover that those time-honored, traditional recipes and old family favorites can be prepared in a fraction of the time that you spent preparing them before. For example, butter and cream cheese can be used directly from the refrigerator. This eliminates the time it takes for them to reach room temperature.

You'll find some familiar recipes in this chapter, but the techniques of assembly have been streamlined. The food processor invites improvisation too, as we discovered when we began experimenting with the light, refreshing fruit ices on page 70.

Carrot Cake

Everyone likes carrot cake and it's a bonus for the cook to be able to prepare it so quickly with a food processor. Use the cream cheese frosting if you bake it in a rectangular baking pan. The orange glaze is best if you bake the cake in a bundt pan.

- 4 medium-size carrots
- ½ cup walnuts or pecans
- 2 cups all-purpose flour, unsifted
- 1½ teaspoons soda
- 2 teaspoons *each* baking powder and ground cinnamon
- 1 teaspoon salt
- 2 cups sugar
- 4 eggs
- 1½ cups salad oil
- 1 can (8 oz.) crushed pineapple, drained
  Cream cheese frosting or orange glaze (recipes follow)

Insert shredding disc and shred carrots; you should have 2 cups. Set aside. Change to metal blade. Process nuts with on-off bursts until coarsely chopped; set aside. Process flour, soda, baking powder, cinnamon, and salt for 2 seconds to mix; transfer to a large mixing bowl. Process sugar and eggs for 15 seconds or until well mixed. Add oil and process for 5 seconds to blend. Pour oil mixture over dry ingredients and mix with a spoon. Stir in shredded carrots, nuts, and pineapple.

Pour batter into a greased and flour-dusted 9 by 13-inch baking pan or a 10-inch bundt pan. Bake in a 350° oven for 45 minutes (55 minutes for bundt pan) or until a wooden pick inserted in center comes out clean. Cool before frosting. If you use a bundt pan, cool cake 15 minutes, then turn out of pan and finish cooling on a wire rack. Makes 12 to 15 servings.

Cream Cheese Frosting. Cut a ½ by 3-inch strip of zest (colored part of peel) from an **orange;** cut zest in quarters. Cut into chunks: 2 packages (3 oz. *each*) **cream cheese** and 6 tablespoons **butter** or margarine. With metal blade in place, turn on food processor. Drop zest and chunks of cream cheese and butter through feed tube and process until zest is finely chopped. Add 1 teaspoon **vanilla** and 2 cups **powdered sugar** and process until blended. Scrape sides of processor bowl with spatula, then process 10 seconds to blend. Makes enough to frost a 9 by 13-inch cake.

Orange Glaze. Cut a ½ by 3-inch strip of zest (colored part of peel) from an **orange** and cut in thin strips. Using metal blade, process zest, 2 cups **powdered sugar**, 1 teaspoon **vanilla,** and 3 tablespoons **orange juice** until zest is finely chopped. Drizzle frosting over cake.

Apple Cake

The apple flavor is very, very fresh in this moist and slightly chewy cake. Serve it warm or cooled with a dusting of powdered sugar, or a topping of whipped cream or vanilla ice cream.

2 cups all-purpose flour, unsifted
2 teaspoons soda
1 teaspoon *each* salt, ground nutmeg, and
   ground cinnamon
1 cup walnuts
4 large, tart apples
½ cup (¼ lb.) butter or margarine
2 cups sugar
2 eggs
1 teaspoon vanilla
¾ cup raisins

Using metal blade, process flour, soda, salt, nutmeg, and cinnamon for 2 seconds to mix; transfer to a large mixing bowl. Process walnuts with on-off bursts until coarsely chopped; add to flour.

Peel and core apples and cut in chunks. Process 2 apples at a time with on-off bursts until coarsely chopped; you should have 4 cups. Set aside.

Cut butter in chunks and process with sugar for 30 seconds or until creamy. Add eggs and process for 30 seconds. Scrape bowl with a spatula, add vanilla, and process for 30 seconds or until smooth and light. Add to flour mixture and stir until blended. Add chopped apples and raisins and stir until mixed (batter will be stiff).

Spoon into a greased 9 by 13-inch baking pan and spread in an even layer. Bake in a 350° oven for 45 minutes or until a wooden pick inserted in center comes out clean. Makes 12 to 15 servings.

Date Cake

This is a long-time favorite *Sunset* recipe streamlined for assembly in the food processor. The cake freezes well; but for a freshly baked flavor, warm the frozen cake and serve it topped with whipped cream or ice cream.

1 cup water
½ teaspoon soda
1 cup pitted dates
1½ cups all-purpose flour, unsifted
1 teaspoon baking powder
½ teaspoon ground cinnamon
¼ teaspoon salt
½ cup (¼ lb.) butter or margarine
1 cup sugar
2 eggs
1 teaspoon vanilla
   Date frosting (recipe follows)

In a small pan, bring water to a boil. Add soda and stir until dissolved; then add dates and cool. (Occasionally, packaged pitted dates have an undetected pit. Check to be sure they are all removed, as a pit could become wedged between the processor bowl and blade.)

Using metal blade, process flour, baking powder, cinnamon, and salt for 2 seconds to mix; set aside. Cut butter in small chunks. Process butter and

sugar until creamy. Add eggs and process for 30 seconds. Scrape sides of bowl with a spatula, then process for 1 minute or until light and creamy. Add flour mixture and process with 3 on-off bursts. Pour off cooled date water into batter and process with 2 on-off bursts. Add vanilla and dates and process with 2 on-off bursts or just until dates are chopped. Do not overprocess.

Pour into a greased 9-inch-square pan and bake in a 350° oven for 40 minutes or until a wooden pick inserted in center comes out clean. Cool cake in pan, then cover with frosting. Makes 9 to 12 servings.

Date Frosting. Using metal blade, process ½ cup pitted **dates** and ½ cup **walnuts** with on-off bursts until coarsely chopped. In a 3-quart pan, bring 1 cup **water** and ½ cup *each* firmly packed **brown sugar** and **granulated sugar** to boiling. Reduce heat to medium-low and, stirring occasionally, cook for 10 minutes. Add date-nut mixture and ½ cup (¼ lb.) **butter** or margarine. Continue cooking, stirring, until frosting thickens slightly when dripped off a spoon. Pour over cake. Let frosting cool before cutting cake. (Frosting will be slightly runny but will set after it cools.)

Pecan Zweiback Torte

(Pictured on page 72)

When you process nuts, there is a point — just before the nuts turn into a butter — when they become mealy. This quality makes it possible to use them as a major ingredient in baking where they can take the place of flour. Here, pecans supply the body for this tender, rich layer cake.

1½ cups pecans
10 pieces zweiback
5 eggs
1 cup sugar
1 teaspoon vanilla
1 teaspoon baking powder
½ teaspoon salt
1 cup whipping cream
   Sugar
⅓ cup raspberry jam
12 pecan halves for garnish

Heavily butter and flour-dust 2 cake pans, 8 or 9 inches in diameter. Using metal blade, process pecans until very finely chopped and mealy; set aside. Break each piece of zweiback in half. With processor running, drop zweiback through the feed tube, a few pieces at a time, and process to make fine crumbs; you should have ¾ cup. Add to nuts. Process eggs, sugar, and vanilla for 1 minute. Add baking powder and salt and process with 1 on-off burst. Add nut-crumb mixture and process for 2 seconds to blend.

Pour ½ of batter into each prepared cake pan and

spread evenly. Bake in a 350° oven for 25 to 30 minutes or just until cake begins to pull away from sides of pan. Let cake cool in pans for 5 minutes, then invert on wire racks to cool.

Whip cream until stiff, sweeten with sugar to taste. Place 1 cake layer on serving dish, cover with ½ of the jam, then cover with ½ of the whipped cream. Top with second cake layer, cover with remaining jam, then top with remaining whipped cream. Decorate top with pecan halves. Cut and serve, or chill as long as overnight. Makes 10 to 12 servings.

Pineapple Bran Bread

(Pictured on page 72)

This quick fruit bread stays moist and fresh for several days.

    1 cup walnuts or pecans
    2 cups all-purpose flour, unsifted
    3 teaspoons baking powder
    ½ teaspoon soda
    ¾ teaspoon salt
    3 tablespoons butter or margarine
    ¾ cup sugar
    1 egg
    1½ cups crushed pineapple, undrained
    1 cup bran cereal

Using metal blade, process nuts with on-off bursts until chopped; set aside. Process flour, baking powder, soda, and salt for 2 seconds to mix; set aside. Cut butter in chunks. Process butter and sugar for 15 seconds or until well mixed. Add egg and process for 30 seconds to blend (mixture will look like a soft batter). Add flour mixture and pineapple and process with 2 on-off bursts. Add nuts and bran and process with 3 on-off bursts or just until mixed. Do not overprocess.

Turn into a greased 9 by 5-inch loaf pan. Bake in a 350° oven for 1 hour or until a wooden pick inserted in center comes out clean. (If you bake bread in small loaves as shown in the photograph, reduce baking time to 40 to 45 minutes.) Let cool before slicing. Makes 1 large loaf or 3 small loaves.

Peanut Pie

This peanut-flavored meringue shell is wonderfully delicious and a breeze to make. Add the whipped-cream filling just before serving.

    20 round (1¾ inches) butter crackers
    ¾ cup salted peanuts
    1 cup sugar
    3 egg whites
    ¼ teaspoon cream of tartar
    1 cup whipping cream

Using metal blade, process crackers to make fine crumbs (about 2 minutes). Add nuts and ½ cup of the sugar to crumbs and process for 5 seconds or until nuts are finely chopped but not powdered.

Using electric mixer or rotary beater, beat egg whites to form soft peaks. Sprinkle in cream of tartar and beat. Continue beating, adding the remaining ½ cup sugar a little at a time, until meringue is stiff and glossy. Fold nut mixture into meringue.

Spoon into an ungreased 9-inch pie pan, shaping mixture so it resembles a pastry shell. Bake in a 325° oven for 25 minutes or until meringue is firm on the outside. Cool for 1 hour (meringue will sink slightly in the middle).

To serve, whip cream, sweeten if desired, and spoon into meringue shell. Makes 6 to 8 servings.

Chocolate Cheesecake Squares

Squares of this cheesecake are firm enough to eat like cookies. To serve attractively, nestle each square in a tiny foil cupcake liner.

    1 cup all-purpose flour, unsifted
    ½ cup sugar
    3 tablespoons cocoa
    1 teaspoon baking powder
    ¼ teaspoon salt
    ½ cup (¼ lb.) butter or margarine
    1 egg, separated
    1 teaspoon vanilla
    ½ cup walnuts
       Cheesecake filling (recipe follows)
    1 square (1 oz.) semisweet chocolate

Line the bottom and two opposite sides of a 9-inch square pan with a strip of foil that overlaps the sides of the pan; grease foil and all pan sides.

Using metal blade, process flour, sugar, cocoa, baking powder, and salt for 2 seconds. Cut butter into chunks. While processor is running, drop chunks down feed tube, 1 at a time, and process until mixture looks like cornmeal. Add egg yolk (save white for filling), vanilla, and nuts, and process until mixture forms a ball and nuts are coarsely chopped. Press mixture into prepared pan. Bake in a 325° oven for 15 minutes. Remove crust from oven, let cool 5 minutes, then slowly pour cheesecake filling over crust. Return to oven and continue baking for 20 minutes or until filling is set.

Cool in pan for 1 hour, then garnish top with chocolate curls made by scraping the square of chocolate (at room temperature) with a vegetable peeler. Cover and chill well.

To serve, lift cheesecake from pan with foil sling, then cut in small squares. Makes 25 pieces.

Cheesecake Filling. Cut a ½ by 3-inch strip of zest (colored part of peel) from an **orange;** cut zest in quarters. Using metal blade, process zest and ⅓ cup **sugar** until zest is finely chopped. Cut 1 large package (8 oz.) **cream cheese** in chunks, add to sugar, and process until creamy. Add ½-cup **sour cream**, 1 tablespoon **flour**, ¼ teaspoon **salt**, ½ teaspoon **vanilla**, 1 **egg**, and reserved **egg white**. Process until smooth.

Slim-line Cheesecake

The food processor is ideal for mixing cheesecake, and here is a low calorie version without a crust. Garnish it with sliced strawberries or other fresh fruit. Or, if you're not counting calories, top it with almond praline.

  1 cup unflavored yogurt
  ½ by 2-inch strip lemon zest (colored part of the peel)
  1 cup sugar
  4 cups low fat cottage cheese
  5 eggs
  3 tablespoons all-purpose flour
  2 teaspoons vanilla
     Sliced strawberries or almond praline for garnish (recipe follows)

Place yogurt in a large mixing bowl. Tear zest in thirds. Using metal blade, process zest and sugar until zest is finely chopped; add to yogurt. Process cottage cheese, eggs, flour, and vanilla until smooth. Add to yogurt and stir well.

Pour into a buttered 9-inch-square pan. Bake in a 325° oven for 40 minutes or until cheesecake just begins to pull away from edges of pan. Center should be slightly jiggly (it sets as it cools). Chill. Garnish as desired. Makes 12 to 16 servings.

Almond Praline. In a frying pan, heat 2 teaspoons **butter** or margarine and 3 tablespoons **sugar** over medium-high heat. When it bubbles, add ¾ cup slivered blanched **almonds**. Cook, stirring, until nuts turn golden. Spread on a sheet of foil and let cool. Break into several pieces and drop into food processor fitted with metal blade. Process with on-off bursts until coarsely chopped. Makes ¾ cup.

Cream Puffs

(Pictured on page 72)

Pâte à chou or chou paste is very versatile. You can make it into cream puffs for dessert or cocktail-size puffs for hors d'oeuvres; or you might spread it on chicken for a dramatic topping (page 45); and there are a dozen other uses. If you have ever made cream puff pastry, you know that it takes a lot of strenuous beating to incorporate the eggs into the cooked flour mixture. The food processor does it for you in seconds.

  1 cup water
  ½ cup (¼ lb.) butter or margarine
  ¼ teaspoon salt
  1 teaspoon sugar (use only for dessert puffs)
  1 cup all-purpose flour, unsifted
  4 eggs

In a 3-quart pan, bring water, butter, salt, and sugar (if used) to a boil. When butter melts, remove pan from heat and add flour all at once. Beat until well blended.

Return pan to medium heat and stir rapidly for 1 minute or until a ball forms in the middle of the pan and a film forms on bottom of pan.

Spoon mixture into food processor bowl fitted with metal blade. Add 2 of the eggs and process until well blended. Add remaining 2 eggs and process until well mixed (about 30 seconds).

Shape and bake chou paste (directions follow) while it is still warm and pliable. If you wish to refrigerate it, cover with plastic wrap, but be sure to let it stand at room temperature for 1 hour before baking. Makes about 2 cups.

To shape and bake cream puffs. Shape cream puffs with pastry bag or spoon using 2 tablespoons chou paste for large puffs, 1 tablespoon for medium-size puffs, and 1½ teaspoons for cocktail-size puffs. Place 2 inches apart on greased baking sheet. Beat 1 **egg** with 1 teaspoon **water**. Brush egg glaze over top of puffs, being sure glaze does not dribble down sides onto baking sheet (this prevents proper rising of puffs).

Bake in upper third of a 425° oven for 15 minutes. Reduce heat to 375° and bake for 5 minutes more. Cut a slash in bottom of each puff and continue baking for 10 minutes or until puffs are firm, dry to touch, and golden brown. Cool on wire racks. Wrap airtight and freeze if you want to store for longer than 24 hours. Makes about 2 dozen large puffs, 3 dozen medium-size puffs, or 5 dozen cocktail-size puffs.

To serve dessert cream puffs. Split cream puffs and fill with crème frangipane (recipe follows), or fill with sweetened whipped cream; dust tops with powdered sugar. Or fill puffs with ice cream and serve with a sauce. (Cream puffs filled with ice cream can be frozen ahead of time; remove from freezer 10 minutes before serving.) You could use vanilla, coffee, or peppermint ice cream as a filling and top with chocolate sauce.

Crème Frangipane. In a small pan, mix ⅓ cup **sugar** with 1 tablespoon **cornstarch** and ⅔ cup **milk**. Bring to a boil, stirring, until thickened and smooth. Remove sauce from heat and at once stir in 1 **egg yolk** (save white for other uses). Flavor sauce with 1½ tablespoons **kirsch** or 1 teaspoon **vanilla**. (Cover pan and chill sauce as long as 2 days, if you like.) Beat ⅓ cup **whipping cream** until stiff and fold into cooled sauce. Makes enough to fill 8 medium-size cream puffs.

Almond Tartlets

(Pictured on page 73)

These miniature tarts look complicated but are surprisingly simple to prepare. The filling starts with canned almond paste. The butter pastry handles easily and can be used for many different desserts. You could roll it out to fit two 9-inch tart pans, bake them blind (empty), and fill the shells with fresh fruit of the season.

2½ cups all-purpose flour, unsifted
⅓ cup sugar
1 cup (½ lb.) butter or margarine, at refrigerator temperature
1 egg
1 teaspoon vanilla
½ teaspoon grated lemon peel
   Frangipane filling (recipe follows)
½ cup sliced almonds
½ cup apricot jam (optional)

Place flour and sugar in food processor fitted with metal blade. Cut butter in small chunks and distribute over flour. Process with on-off bursts until mixture looks mealy. Mix egg, vanilla, and lemon peel. Add to flour mixture and process until dough forms a ball. Remove dough, wrap in plastic wrap, and chill for 10 minutes while you prepare filling.

On a lightly floured board, roll out pastry, ½ at a time, to ⅛ inch thickness. Cut out 2-inch circles. Fit each circle into tiny fluted tartlet pans or tiny muffin pans. Spoon 1½ teaspoons filling into each tartlet and sprinkle a few almond slices over each. Bake in a 350° oven until filling is firm and pastry is lightly browned (10 to 12 minutes). Let cool for 10 minutes before removing from pans.

If desired, heat apricot jam over low heat, then spoon a little jam on the top of each cooled tartlet. Makes about 4½ dozen tartlets.

Frangipane Filling. Coarsely crumble ¾ cup (6 oz.) **almond paste** into processor bowl fitted with metal blade. Add ½ cup **sugar**, 1½ teaspoons *each* rum and **vanilla**, 2 tablespoons softened **butter** or margarine, and 3 **eggs.** Process until mixture is smooth and creamy (1 to 2 minutes).

Mock Puff Pastry

This is a simple way to make puff paste without having to butter, fold, roll, and chill the dough many times — the way French bakers traditionally do it. Puff pastry has many uses; we give directions for shaping it three ways. To make a sweet pastry, roll the dough in granulated sugar. To make an hors d'oeuvre or salad accompaniment, roll the dough in grated parmesan cheese and sprinkle with your favorite herb.

2 cups all-purpose flour, unsifted
1 cup (½ lb.) butter, at refrigerator temperature
½ cup sour cream
1 egg yolk

Place flour in processor bowl fitted with metal blade. Cut butter in ½-inch chunks and distribute over flour. Process with on-off bursts until butter particles range from the size of dried beans to peas.

Mix sour cream and egg yolk. Add to flour mixture and process just until mixture begins to form a ball. (Do not process completely to the ball stage, and don't worry if there are streaks in dough.) Remove dough, divide in half, wrap in plastic wrap, and chill for at least 1 hour or as long as 3 days. Freeze for longer storage. Roll out and bake according to the following directions. If dough starts to crack, it means the butter is too hard; let dough stand 10 minutes to soften slightly before rolling.

Palm Leaves. On a board lightly coated with **granulated sugar** or grated **Parmesan cheese,** roll out 1 of the chilled puff pastry dough halves to form a rectangle 8 by 18 inches and ⅛ inch thick. Sprinkle more sugar (or cheese and your favorite herb) over pastry and press in lightly with rolling pin.

Fold each of the 2 long sides 1⅓ inches toward the center. Fold each long side again 1⅓ inches toward center so folds meet in center. Fold dough again, in half toward the center, to make a compact 6 layer roll. Cover with plastic wrap and chill for 1 hour. If you don't wish to bake pastries within an hour, freeze. (If left in refrigerator more than 1 hour the sugar begins to dissolve.)

To bake, cut chilled or frozen pastry crosswise in ¼-inch slices and place on baking sheet, cut side up, allowing 1½ inches between each slice. Bake in a 400° oven for 10 minutes (12 minutes if frozen) or until lightly browned. Cool on wire rack. Makes 3 dozen palm leaf pastries.

Sweet Twists. Mix ½ cup **granulated sugar** and 1 teaspoon **ground cinnamon.** Sprinkle half of mixture lightly on counter. Roll out ½ of chilled puff pastry dough on counter to form an 8 by 18-inch rectangle that is ⅛-inch thick. Sprinkle remainder of sugar mixture over pastry and press in lightly with rolling pin.

Cut pastry crosswise in ½-inch-wide strips. Holding each end of strip, twist it 5 times. Place each twisted strip on baking sheet; press each end down on sheet (to secure twist while baking). Repeat until baking sheet is filled.

Bake in a 400° oven for 10 minutes or until pastries are lightly browned. Remove from oven and cut each strip in half while it is still warm. Cool on wire racks. Makes 6 dozen 4-inch twists.

Sweet Pretzels. On a board lightly coated with **granulated sugar,** roll out ½ of chilled puff pastry dough to form an 8 by 18-inch rectangle that is ⅛ inch thick. Lightly sprinkle more sugar over pastry. Cut pastry crosswise in ¼-inch-wide strips. Shape each strip into a pretzel shape, then place on baking sheet. Bake in a 400° oven for 10 minutes or until lightly browned. Makes 6 dozen pretzels.

Crumb Crust

Graham crackers, zweiback, vanilla or chocolate wafers, and gingersnaps can be made into crumbs quickly with the food processor to make crumb crusts.

Fit processor with metal blade. Break **crackers or cookies** into pieces to fit the feed tube, drop in a few pieces at a time, and process enough to make 1½ cups fine crumbs (see Conversion Table, page 9).

To crumbs, add ⅓ cup **butter** or margarine cut in small chunks and ¼ cup **sugar**; process until well mixed. (Omit sugar if you use cooky crumbs.)

Press mixture firmly onto bottom and sides of a 9-inch pie pan. Chill for at least 1 hour or, for a firmer crust, bake in a 350° oven for 10 minutes.

Rich Pie Pastry

This pastry has all the right qualities. It is both flaky and tender; it is easy to roll out, and the flavor is delicious. Use the pastry dough for any pie or quiche, or as a wrapping for hors d'oeuvre turnovers.

Because the food processor works so rapidly, it is important to start with frozen butter and shortening so the fat remains in particles and is not creamed. This ensures a flaky pastry.

- 1¼ cups all-purpose flour, unsifted
- ¼ teaspoon salt
- ¼ cup *frozen* shortening (remove from measuring cup before freezing)
- ¼ cup *frozen* butter
- 3 tablespoons ice water

Place flour and salt in processor bowl fitted with metal blade. Cut shortening and butter in ½-inch chunks and distribute over flour. Process until fat particles look like small peas (8 seconds). Measure water into a cup, turn motor on again, and add water slowly through feed tube. Turn off motor. Mixture will look crumbly. Do not allow mixture to form a ball. (If dough accidentally forms a ball, you can still use it, but pastry will not be as flaky.)

Turn mixture out onto a square of plastic wrap and pull up corners of plastic shaping dough to form a 4-inch-wide patty. Cover and refrigerate for 1 hour. (This allows the dough to rest, so do not speed the chilling by placing dough in the freezer.)

Roll dough out on a lightly floured board to ⅛-inch thickness. Fit loosely into a 9 or 10-inch pie pan and crimp edges. Prick bottom and sides with a fork. Bake in a 425° oven until lightly browned (about 12 to 15 minutes). Makes enough pastry for a single-crust 9 or 10-inch pie. Double recipe for a 2-crust pie.

Cream Cheese Kolache Pastries

(Pictured on page 73)

Choose dried apricots or prunes to make the filling for these good looking pastries.

- 3 cups all-purpose flour, unsifted
- 1 teaspoon baking powder
- ½ teaspoon salt
- 1 cup (½ lb.) butter or margarine
- 1 large package (8 oz.) cream cheese
- ½ cup sugar
- 1 teaspoon vanilla
- 2 eggs
  Apricot or prune filling (recipe follows)
  Granulated sugar

Using metal blade, process flour, baking powder, and salt for 2 seconds to mix; set aside. Cut butter and cream cheese into small chunks. With processor running, drop chunks through feed tube and process until smooth and creamy. Add sugar and process until well blended. Add vanilla and eggs and process for 1 minute or until well mixed.

Add flour mixture, ½ at a time, and process until mixture is well blended. Stop processor several times and scrape sides of bowl with spatula. Divide dough in half, wrap each portion, and chill until firm (at least 3 hours or overnight).

Remove 1 portion of dough at a time from refrigerator. Roll dough on a lightly floured board into a 12 by 15-inch rectangle; cut dough into 3-inch squares. Spread a slightly rounded teaspoon of apricot or prune filling on each square in a diagonal strip to within ¼ inch of 2 opposite corners. Fold the 2 corners without filling into the middle so they overlap. Press top gently to seal the overlap.

Sprinkle pastries very lightly with sugar. Transfer to ungreased cooky sheets and bake in a 325° oven for about 25 minutes or until edges are lightly browned. With spatula, transfer pastries to wire racks to cool. Makes 40 pastries.

Apricot or Prune Filling. Place 1 cup **dried apricots** or pitted prunes in a small pan with ½ cup **water**, ¾ cup **sugar**, ½ teaspoon grated **lemon peel**, 1 tablespoon **lemon juice**, ¼ teaspoon **ground cinnamon**, and ⅛ teaspoon **ground cloves.** Bring to simmering over medium heat, then reduce heat, cover, and simmer for 5 minutes.

Remove from heat and cool for 10 minutes. Process with metal blade until very finely chopped but not puréed. You should have about 1¼ cups. If necessary, return to pan and stir over low heat until reduced to 1¼ cups or stir in water to bring to this measure. Makes filling for 40 pastries.

Pirouettes (Curled Cookies)

(Pictured on page 72-73)

These cookies become crisp as they cool, so bake only four at a time and roll them while they are still warm. Each batch bakes quickly in 3 minutes.

- 6 tablespoons butter or margarine
- 1 cup powdered sugar
- ⅔ cup all-purpose flour, unsifted
- ½ teaspoon grated lemon peel
- 1 teaspoon vanilla
- 4 egg whites

Cut butter in chunks. Using metal blade, process butter and powdered sugar until creamy. Add flour and lemon peel and process for 30 seconds. Add vanilla and egg whites and process until batter is smooth (about 1 minute).

Spoon 1½ teaspoons batter on a well-greased baking sheet, then spread thinly with a spatula or knife to make a rectangle about 3 by 4 inches. Repeat to make 3 more cookies. Bake in a 425° oven for 3 minutes or until edges begin to brown. Remove from oven and quickly roll each cooky lengthwise around a wooden spoon handle or chopstick to form a scroll. Slide cooky off of spoon handle and cool on wire rack. Repeat, baking and rolling 4 cookies at a time, until all batter is used. To retain crispness, store in a tightly covered container. Makes 3 dozen cookies.

Mexican Tea Cakes

You can vary the flavor of these cookies by using different nuts, but no matter what variety of nut you use, the cookies melt in your mouth.

- 1 cup walnuts, blanched almonds, filberts, or macadamia nuts
- ½ cup (¼ lb.) butter or margarine
- 1 tablespoon sugar
- 1 cup all-purpose flour, unsifted
- 1 teaspoon vanilla
- Powdered sugar

Using metal blade, process nuts with on-off bursts until finely chopped; set aside. Cut butter in small chunks. With motor running, drop chunks down feed tube and process until creamy. Add sugar and process for 2 seconds. Add flour and process until mixture forms a ball. Add vanilla and nuts and process just until blended (about 5 seconds).

Roll dough into balls 1 inch in diameter and place on a lightly greased baking sheet. Bake in a 325° oven for 30 minutes or until firm and very lightly browned. While still hot, roll in powdered sugar until coated on all sides. Place on a wire rack to cool. Makes 3 dozen cookies.

Peanut Butter Cookies

Wheat germ gives a special nutlike flavor to these cookies. As you read the sequence of steps in the directions, you can see how a favorite recipe can be adapted for quick preparation with the food processor.

- 1½ cups all-purpose flour, unsifted
- ½ cup wheat germ
- ½ teaspoon *each* salt and soda
- ½ cup (¼ lb.) butter or margarine
- ¾ cup firmly packed brown sugar
- ¼ cup honey
- 1 egg
- 1 teaspoon vanilla
- 1 cup chunk-style peanut butter

Using metal blade, process flour, wheat germ, salt, and soda for 2 seconds to mix; set aside. Cut butter in chunks. Process butter and brown sugar until creamy. Add honey, egg, vanilla, and peanut butter, and process for 3 seconds. Add flour mixture and process until dough is blended.

Roll dough, a tablespoon at a time, into balls; place 3 inches apart on greased cooky sheets. Flatten balls with a fork. Bake in a 325° oven for 15 minutes or until edges are lightly browned. Makes about 4 dozen cookies.

Chocolate Mint Bars

These confection-like cookies deliciously combine chocolate and mint.

- 3 squares (1 oz. *each*) unsweetened chocolate
- ½ cup (¼ lb.) plus 1 tablespoon butter or margarine
- Hot water
- 2 eggs
- 1 cup sugar
- ½ cup all-purpose flour, unsifted
- ¼ teaspoon salt
- 1 teaspoon vanilla
- ½ cup walnuts
- Peppermint frosting (recipe follows)

Melt 2 squares of the chocolate and the ½ cup butter over hot water. Using metal blade, process eggs and sugar for 30 seconds. Add chocolate-butter mixture and process for 5 seconds or until blended. Add flour, salt, vanilla, and nuts and process with on-off bursts until well mixed and nuts are chopped. Spoon into a greased 9-inch square baking pan and spread evenly. Bake in a 350° oven for 20

(Continued on page 70)

GLISTENING CRYSTALLINE ICES capture the essence of fresh fruits at their peak. Clockwise, from upper left: strawberry, papaya, pineapple, raspberry, and orange Fresh Fruit Ices (page 70).

minutes or until a wooden pick inserted in center comes out clean. Cool.

Spread peppermint frosting on top. Chill in refrigerator for 30 minutes or until frosting hardens. Melt the remaining 1 square chocolate with the 1 tablespoon butter over hot water. Drizzle melted chocolate over frosting. Refrigerate until chocolate is firm, then cut in small squares. Makes 2 dozen cookies.

Peppermint Frosting. Cut 2 tablespoons **butter** or margarine in chunks. Using metal blade, process until creamy. Add 1 tablespoon **whipping cream** or half-and-half (light cream),½ teaspoon **peppermint extract,** and 1 cup **powdered sugar,** and process until smooth.

Chocolate Mousse

This smooth chocolaty dessert is so rich, it's best to serve it in small quantities. It uses sweet butter, which is often found in the frozen food section of supermarkets because it is more perishable than salted butter.

> 4 ounces semisweet chocolate or ¾ cup
> chocolate pieces
> ½ cup (¼ lb.) sweet butter
> 6 tablespoons sugar
> 3 eggs

Melt chocolate over hot water. Cut butter in ½-inch chunks. Fit metal blade in food processor and turn motor on. Drop butter, a few pieces at a time, through feed tube and process until smooth. Add sugar and process until creamy (about 1 minute). Add melted chocolate and process for 15 seconds. Scrape sides of bowl with spatula and process for 15 more seconds. Add eggs, 1 at a time, and process for 15 seconds after each addition.

Spoon into small individual serving dishes, cover, and chill. Makes 6 servings.

Fresh Fruit Ices

(Pictured on page 69)

This refreshing fruit ice is lighter than ice cream, cooler than sherbet, and packed with fresh fruit flavor. Best of all — it is so simple to prepare. We have included recipes for seven varieties of ice to get you started, but you can experiment with any other fruit or combination of fruits, if you wish.

Process fresh fruit or berries of the season to make a purée (see individual ices at right). Freeze purée in divided ice cube trays. When purée is frozen, you can transfer cubes to plastic bags; return to freezer.

To serve, use metal blade to process 4 to 6 cubes of purée at a time. Use on-off bursts at first to break up cubes, then run processor continually until you have a velvety slush. Spoon into serving containers and serve at once. You might choose to serve the ice in a clear glass to show off the sparkling natural color of the ice, or present it in a fruit shell from half an orange, grapefruit, or pineapple. If you wish to serve a large quantity, return ices in their serving containers to freezer until you have processed desired number of servings.

Raspberry Ice. Using metal blade, process 4 cups **raspberries** until puréed. Pour through a sieve and discard seeds. Return purée to processor along with ¾ cup **sugar,** 1 tablespoon **lemon juice,** and ½ cup **water.** (If you prefer a less concentrated flavor, add as much as 1 cup water.) Process for 2 seconds to mix. Freeze and serve ice according to preceding directions. Makes about 2¾ cups.

Boysenberry Ice. Using metal blade, process 2 cups **boysenberries** until puréed. Pour through a sieve and discard seeds. Return to processor along with ½ cup **water,** ½ cup **sugar,** and 2 tablespoons **lemon juice.** Process for 2 seconds to mix. Freeze and serve according to preceding directions. Makes 2 cups.

Strawberry Ice. Using metal blade, process 4 cups **strawberries** until puréed. Add ½ cup **sugar,** ½ cup **water,** and 1 tablespoon **lemon juice.** Process for 2 seconds to mix. Freeze and serve according to preceding directions. Makes 3 cups.

Pineapple Ice. Peel and core 1 large **pineapple;** cut in chunks. Using metal blade, process ½ at a time until puréed; you should have 4 cups. Pour purée into a bowl and stir in 1 cup **water,** ¼ cup **sugar,** and 2 tablespoons **lemon juice.** (If pineapple makes slightly less or more than 4 cups purée, adjust sugar proportion to taste.) Freeze and serve according to preceding directions. Makes 5 cups.

Papaya Ice. Peel 1 large **papaya,** cut in half, remove seeds, and quarter. Using metal blade, process until puréed; you should have 1¼ cups. Add 2 tablespoons **lemon juice,** 3 tablespoons **honey,** and ⅓ cup **water.** Process for 2 seconds to mix. Freeze and serve according to preceding directions. Makes 1⅔ cups.

Lemon Ice. Remove zest (colored part of peel) from 1 small **lemon** and cut in ½-inch pieces. Using metal blade, process zest and 1 cup **sugar** until zest is finely chopped. Place in a 3-quart pan with 4 cups **water** and a dash of **salt.** Heat just until sugar dissolves. Let cool, then stir in ⅔ cup **lemon juice.** Freeze and serve according to preceding directions. Makes about 4½ cups.

Orange Ice. From an **orange,** cut a ½ by 3-inch strip of zest (colored part of peel) in ½-inch pieces. Using metal blade, process zest with ¾ cup **sugar** until finely chopped. Place in a small pan with 1 cup **water** and heat until sugar dissolves. Let cool, then stir in 1½ cups **orange juice** and 2 tablespoons **lemon juice.** Freeze and serve according to preceding directions. Makes about 3 cups.

Brioches and Croissants

The food processor is not designed to handle large quantities of yeast dough. But for those times when you don't want to get involved in full-scale baking, you can use it to make small batches of special breads.

Petites Brioches

(Pictured on page 26)

Rich in eggs and butter, brioches are certainly elegant fare.

 1 package active dry yeast
 ½ cup warm water (about 110°)
 2 teaspoons sugar
 1¼ teaspoons salt
 3 eggs
 ½ cup (¼ lb.) butter or margarine, at room temperature
    About 3½ cups all-purpose flour, unsifted
 1 egg yolk beaten with 1 tablespoon milk

Using metal blade, process yeast and water with 2 on-off bursts; let stand 5 minutes. Add sugar, salt, and eggs, and process for 2 seconds. Cut butter in small pieces and add to eggs along with 3⅓ cups of the flour. Process just until dough holds together (about 4 seconds; if processor begins to slow down, turn off motor.) Turn dough onto a board and knead lightly 25 times, adding up to ¼ cup flour to prevent sticking. Dough should be smooth and satiny.

Turn dough over in a greased bowl; cover and let rise in a warm place until doubled (1 to 2 hours). Punch dough down; knead briefly on a floured board. Return to greased bowl; turn over to grease top. Cover with plastic wrap; refrigerate for 12 to 24 hours.

Knead on a lightly floured board to release air. Divide dough into 12 equal portions if using 3 to 4-inch petite brioche pans or 3-inch muffin cups; 16 equal portions if using 2½-inch muffin cups. Dough is easiest to handle if kept cold, so shape a few at a time, keeping remaining dough covered and refrigerated.

Pinch off about ⅙ of each portion; set aside. Shape large section into a smooth ball by pulling surface of dough to underside of ball. Set ball, smooth side up, in a well-buttered petite brioche pan or muffin cup. Press dough down to fill pan bottom evenly. Shape a small piece of dough into a teardrop that is smooth.

With your finger, poke a hole in center of brioche dough in pan and insert pointed end of teardrop, settling it securely (or it may pop off at an angle while baking). Repeat until all brioches are shaped.

Cover filled pans and let stand in a warm place until almost doubled (1 to 2 hours). With brush, paint tops of brioches with egg yolk-milk mixture; do not let glaze accumulate in joint of topknot.

Bake in a 425° oven for 15 to 18 minutes or until richly browned. Remove from pans and serve warm, or let cool on racks. Makes 12 to 16.

Quick Butter Croissants

(Pictured on page 60)

Processing firm butter into flour, then blending the mixture with a yeast batter is a non-traditional but simple way to make flaky croissants.

 5 cups all-purpose flour, unsifted
 1 cup (½ lb.) butter or margarine, at refrigerator temperature
 1 package active dry yeast
 1 cup warm water (about 110°)
 ¾ cup evaporated milk
 1½ teaspoons salt
 ⅓ cup sugar
 1 egg
 ¼ cup butter or margarine, melted and cooled
 1 egg beaten with 1 tablespoon water

Fit metal blade in processor; add 4 cups of the flour. Cut butter in ½-inch squares and distribute over flour. Process, using on-off bursts, until butter particles range from the size of peas to dried beans. Transfer to large mixing bowl.

Process yeast and water with 2 on-off bursts. Add milk, salt, sugar, egg, the remaining 1 cup flour, and melted butter, and process until batter is smooth. Pour over butter-flour mixture. With spatula, carefully turn mixture over just until all flour is moistened. Cover with plastic wrap and refrigerate for at least 4 hours or up to 4 days.

Turn dough onto a floured board, press into a ball, and knead briefly to release air. Divide dough into 4 equal parts. Shape 1 part at a time, leaving remaining dough in refrigerator.

On floured board, roll 1 portion of dough into a 14-inch circle. With sharp knife, cut in 8 equal wedges. Loosely roll each wedge from wide end toward point. Curve into a crescent and place, point-side down, on an ungreased baking sheet. Repeat until all croissants are shaped and placed on baking sheet 1½ inches apart all around. Cover lightly and let rise at room temperature in a draft-free place. (Do not speed rising by placing in warm spot.)

When almost doubled (about 2 hours), brush with egg-water mixture. Bake in a 325° oven for 35 minutes or until lightly browned. Serve warm, or let cool on racks. Makes 32 croissants.

FANCY DESSERTS *are effortlessly made when you use a food processor. Clockwise, from bottom right: Almond Tartlets (page 66), Cream Cheese Kolache Pastries (page 67), Cream Puffs (page 65), Pirouettes (page 68), Pineapple Bran Bread (page 64), Pecan Zweiback Torte (page 63).*

ROLL PIROUETTES, *while still warm and pliable, around chopstick or wooden spoon handle; curled cookies become crisp when cool (page 68).*

SPREAD APRICOT FILLING *in diagonal strip across squares of cooky dough; fold in opposite corners to shape Cream Cheese Kolache Pastries (page 67).*

Preserves & Relishes

The cook who stocks a canning cupboard or freezer with jars of preserves gains a great feeling of satisfaction. Jam, marmalade, fruit butter, chutney, relish, and pickles add zest to meals throughout the year. A bumper crop of tomatoes, turned into an unusual sauce, can speed up meal preparations on later, busy days. It takes time to make preserves, but the job is more enjoyable and takes less time when you do it with a food processor. For more information on canning, see the Sunset book Home Canning.

Carrot-Orange Marmalade

Brilliant-colored marmalade has a crunchy texture when carrots are combined with oranges.

- 6 medium-size carrots
- 2 small oranges
- 3½ cups water
- ¼ cup lemon juice
- ¼ teaspoon ground ginger
- 4 cups sugar

Insert shredding disc and shred carrots; you should have 3 cups. Place in a wide 5 to 6-quart pan. Using a vegetable peeler or paring knife, remove zest (colored part of peel) from oranges; cut zest in thin slivers and add to carrots. Squeeze juice from oranges and add to carrots along with water.

Cover and simmer over low heat for 15 minutes or until zest is tender. Add lemon juice, ginger, and sugar. Bring to a boil, then boil, uncovered, over medium-high heat, stirring frequently, until mixture thickens (about 20 minutes). Can as directed below. Makes about 2 pints.

Canning directions. Place canning jars in boiling water for 15 minutes; then keep hot until ready to use. Scald lids and ring bands; keep in very hot water until ready to use. Ladle hot marmalade into hot jars to within ½ inch of top. Wipe rims with clean, damp cloth. Seal each jar as filled, with a lid and ring band, screwing down the band just as tight as is comfortable. Let cool on a towel away from any draft. Leave on ring band until the jar is cool to touch. Test for a good seal; press lid with your finger. If it stays down, jar is sealed.

Spiced Apple Honey Butter

Simple fruit purée, cooked down to concentrate natural fruit sugars, is delicious on muffins or morning toast. It is not necessary to peel the apples; the skins disappear after cooking and puréeing. The butter can be stored in the refrigerator for as long as three months and frozen for longer storage.

- 4 pounds (about 12 medium-size) tart apples
- 1 cup water
- 1 quart apple juice
- ¼ cup lemon juice
- ½ teaspoon salt
- 2 teaspoons ground cinnamon
- ½ teaspoon ground cloves
- ¼ teaspoon *each* ground ginger and nutmeg
- 1½ cups light, mild-flavored honey

Quarter and core unpeeled apples. In a 6-quart or larger pan, combine apples, water, apple juice, and lemon juice. Cover and simmer over medium-low heat until fruit is soft (about 30 minutes). Using metal blade, process mixture, a portion at a time, until puréed.

Return purée to pan. Add salt, cinnamon, cloves, ginger, nutmeg, and honey. Cook, uncovered, over low heat for 1 to 1½ hours, stirring more frequently as butter thickens. Makes about 3 pints.

To can butter, follow directions under Carrot-Orange Marmalade (at left).

To freeze butter, spoon cooled butter into freezer containers or jars to within 1 inch of top. Cover and freeze.

Ginger-Pear Honey Butter

Fresh pears and ginger team up with honey for a piquant spread to use the year around.

    4 pounds (about 8 large) Bartlett pears
    ¼ cup lemon juice
    ½ teaspoon salt
    ¾ teaspoon ground ginger
    1½ teaspoons grated lemon peel
    1 cup light, mild-flavored honey

Quarter and core unpeeled pears. In a 6-quart or larger pan, combine pears and lemon juice. Cook, covered, over medium-low heat, stirring occasionally, until fruit is soft (about 30 minutes). Using metal blade, process mixture, a portion at a time, until puréed.

Return purée to pan; add salt, ginger, lemon peel, and honey. Cook, uncovered, over low heat for 1½ to 2 hours, stirring more frequently as butter thickens. Makes about 2 pints.

To can butter, follow directions under Carrot-Orange Marmalade (page 74).

To freeze butter, spoon cooled butter into freezer containers or jars to within 1 inch of top. Cover and freeze.

Apricot Chutney

This chutney is medium-hot; for a milder version, omit seeds from the peppers or use fewer peppers.

    1 small clove garlic
    1 medium-size onion
    1 lime
    1 cup *each* granulated sugar, firmly packed
       brown sugar, and cider vinegar
    1 tablespoon finely chopped fresh ginger
       root or ¾ teaspoon ground ginger
    1 teaspoon *each* ground allspice and dry
       mustard
       Dash of ground cloves
    2 small, dried hot chile peppers, crushed
    1 cup currants or raisins
    4 pounds fresh apricots

Using metal blade, process garlic until chopped. Cut onion in chunks, add to garlic, and process with on-off bursts until coarsely chopped. Place in a 4-quart or larger pan. Cut lime in quarters and thinly slice. Add to onion along with granulated and brown sugars, vinegar, ginger, allspice, mustard, cloves, peppers, and currants.

Cut apricots in half and remove pits. Process, a portion at a time, with on-off bursts until coarsely chopped. Bring lime-onion mixture to a boil; then add apricots. Return to boiling, reduce heat, and simmer over medium-low heat until slightly thickened (about 45 minutes). Stir frequently to prevent sticking. Makes 4 pints.

To can chutney, fill jars according to directions under Carrot-Orange Marmalade (page 74); then process in a simmering water bath for 10 minutes.

To freeze chutney, spoon cooled chutney into freezer containers or jars to within 1 inch of top. Cover and freeze.

Fig and Apple Chutney

Sweet-and-sour fig chutney makes a pleasing accompaniment to pork. The figs sweeten the chutney while the apples give it body.

    3 to 3½ pounds fresh figs
    2 pounds tart apples
    1 clove garlic
    1 large onion
    1 lemon
    2 cups cider vinegar
    2⅓ cups firmly packed brown sugar
    ½ teaspoon crushed red pepper
    1½ teaspoons *each* ground allspice and
       cinnamon
    1 teaspoon salt
    ½ teaspoon ground cloves
    1 cup walnuts (optional)

Clip stems from figs. Using metal blade, process figs, a portion at a time, with on-off bursts until coarsely chopped; you should have 6 cups. Place in a 6-quart or larger pan. Peel, core, and quarter apples. Process, a portion at a time, with on-off bursts until coarsely chopped; you should have 6 cups. Add to figs. Process garlic until chopped. Cut onion in chunks, add to garlic, and process with on-off bursts until onion is coarsely chopped. Add to figs.

Cut lemon into quarters and thinly slice; discard seeds. Add to figs along with vinegar, brown sugar, red pepper, allspice, cinnamon, salt, and cloves. Bring to a boil; cook, uncovered, over medium-low heat, stirring frequently until mixture thickens (35 to 40 minutes).

Meanwhile, process walnuts (if desired) with on-off bursts until chopped. Stir into chutney. Makes 6 pints.

To freeze chutney, spoon cooled chutney into freezer containers or jars to within 1 inch of top. Cover and freeze.

Freezer Strawberry Jam

The fresh berry taste is remarkable in this jam. Easy to make and ready to use right from the freezer, it will keep until next year's crop comes around.

(Continued on page 77)

Preserves & Relishes **75**

8 **cups ripe strawberries, hulled**
1 **package (2 oz.) powdered pectin**
1 **cup light corn syrup**
5½ **cups sugar**
4 **tablespoons lemon juice**

Using metal blade, process berries, a portion at a time, until smooth; you should have 4 cups.

Turn puréed strawberries into 2-quart kettle. Stirring vigorously, sift in powdered pectin slowly. Let stand for 20 minutes, stirring strawberries occasionally so pectin thoroughly dissolves. Pour in corn syrup and mix well. Gradually stir in sugar and carefully heat mixture to 100°F. (it should be lukewarm and no hotter).

When sugar is thoroughly dissolved, stir in lemon juice. Ladle jam into jars, cover, and then place in the freezer for 24 hours. (The jam won't freeze solid because of the sugar concentration.) If you want to keep jam longer than one month, keep it in freezer at a temperature range of 10°F below zero to 20° above. Otherwise, you can store it in the refrigerator to use. Makes 4 pints.

Bread and Butter Pickles

(Pictured on facing page)

Soaking sliced cucumbers and onions in a salt-ice cube mixture creates crisp and crunchy pickles. For fastest slicing, choose small cucumbers that will fit in the feed tube. The slim, thin-skinned Oriental varieties are an excellent choice if you grow your own.

About 6 **pounds cucumbers**
8 **small onions**
3 **cloves garlic**
⅓ **cup salt**
6 **to 8 quarts ice cubes**
5 **cups sugar**
3 **cups cider vinegar**
1½ **teaspoons** *each* **turmeric and celery seed**
2 **tablespoons mustard seed**

Wash cucumbers, trim ends, and cut in lengths to fit the feed tube. Insert slicing disc and slice unpeeled cucumbers; you should have 4 quarts. Transfer to a crock or large mixing bowl. Cut onions in half lengthwise, stand in the feed tube, and slice. Add to cucumbers along with whole garlic cloves, salt, and ice. Mix; let stand for 3 hours. Drain thoroughly and remove any ice cubes which have not melted.

PICKLING can be a cool project on a hot summer day. Use your processor to slice onions and cucumbers for Bread and Butter Pickles (recipe above); ice cubes crisp the vegetables before they go into jars.

In an 8-quart kettle, combine sugar, vinegar, turmeric, celery seed, mustard seed, and drained vegetables. Stirring occasionally, heat until boiling.

To can pickles, prepare jars and lids following directions for Carrot-Orange Marmalade (page 74). With a slotted spoon, ladle vegetables into hot jars to within ½ inch of top. Ladle in hot pickling liquid. Wipe rims of jars and seal. Makes 8 pints.

Green Tomato Hamburger Relish

A great way to use up the green tomatoes from your garden, as well as any cucumbers, is to make this relish that is so good on hamburgers and hot dogs.

2 **medium-size cucumbers**
3 **medium-size tart apples**
4 **to 5 medium-size green tomatoes**
4 **medium-size onions**
1 **medium-size green pepper**
2 **small, red bell peppers**
4 **cups water**
1½ **tablespoons salt**
2 **cups** *each* **sugar and cider vinegar**
1 **tablespoon mustard seed**
6 **tablespoons all-purpose flour**
1 **tablespoon dry mustard**
¼ **teaspoon turmeric**

Peel cucumbers and cut into chunks. Peel, core, and quarter apples. Cut green tomatoes and onions into chunks. Cut green pepper and red peppers into chunks and discard seeds. Using metal blade, process vegetables and apples, a portion at a time, with on-off bursts until finely chopped. Place in a 6-quart pan. Stir in water and salt, blending all ingredients. Cover and let stand in refrigerator for 24 hours; drain well.

Add sugar, 1½ cups of the vinegar, and mustard seed; bring to a boil over high heat.

Meanwhile, stir together flour, dry mustard, and turmeric with the remaining ½ cup vinegar. Stir into boiling mixture. Reduce heat and simmer, uncovered, for 1½ hours, or until mixture is quite thick; stir occasionally. Makes about 3 pints.

To can relish, fill jars according to directions under Carrot-Orange Marmalade (page 74); then process in a simmering water bath for 10 minutes.

To freeze relish, spoon cooled relish into freezer containers or jars to within 1 inch of top. Cover and freeze.

Sweet-Sour Chile Sauce

Enjoy homemade chile sauce on grilled beef or lamb patties, or frankfurters. It's a good way to use tomatoes while they are plentiful.

(Continued on next page)

Preserves & Relishes **77**

      4 pounds ripe tomatoes
      1 can (7 oz.) whole California green chiles
      1 small, dried hot chile pepper
      4 large onions
      1 tablespoon salt
      ½ teaspoon ground ginger
      6 tablespoons firmly packed brown sugar
      1 teaspoon ground cinnamon
    1¾ cups white wine vinegar

Peel, core, and quarter tomatoes. Using metal blade, process a portion at a time with on-off bursts until coarsely chopped; you should have 6 cups. Place tomatoes in a 5 to 6-quart pan. Process green chiles and hot chile pepper (remove seeds if desired) with on-off bursts, until coarsely chopped; add to tomatoes.

Cut onions in chunks. Process ½ at a time with on-off bursts until coarsely chopped. Add to tomatoes along with salt, ginger, brown sugar, and cinnamon. Stir to mix well.

Boil gently, uncovered, over medium-low heat until very thick (about 1 hour). Stir frequently as mixture thickens to prevent sticking. Add vinegar and cook 15 to 20 minutes longer. Makes 3 pints.

To freeze sauce, cool sauce, pack into rigid containers to within 1 inch of top. Cover and freeze.

To can sauce, fill jars according to directions for Carrot-Orange Marmalade (page 74); then process in a simmering water bath for 15 minutes.

Freezer Tomato Sauce

This well-seasoned, basic sauce can be served with pasta, broiled beef patties or steaks, shellfish, and vegetables.

      4 cloves garlic
      2 medium-size onions
      ⅓ cup olive oil or salad oil
      5 pounds (about 12 medium-size) ripe
          tomatoes
      1 bunch green onions
      1 green pepper
    1½ teaspoons salt
      ¾ teaspoon pepper
      ¼ teaspoon anise seed, crushed
      1 tablespoon oregano leaves
      ¾ teaspoon rosemary leaves
      1 teaspoon paprika
          About 1¾ cups dry red wine

Using metal blade, process garlic until chopped. Cut onions into chunks, add to garlic, and process with on-off bursts until coarsely chopped. In an 8-quart pan, cook onion and garlic in olive oil over medium heat until golden (about 15 minutes); stir occasionally.

Meanwhile, peel, core, and quarter tomatoes.

Process a portion at a time with on-off bursts until coarsely chopped. Add to cooked onion. Cut green onions and part of the tops into 1-inch lengths. Process with on-off bursts until finely chopped; add to tomato mixture. Cut green pepper in chunks and discard seeds. Process with on-off bursts until coarsely chopped. Add to tomatoes along with salt, pepper, anise seed, oregano, rosemary, paprika, and wine.

Bring mixture to a boil, stirring. Cover, reduce heat, and simmer for 1 hour. Remove cover, increase heat to medium, and boil until mixture is reduced to 8 cups.

You can use sauce while hot, or let it cool and refrigerate for as long as 3 days, or freeze it as long as 4 months.

To freeze sauce, divide it into 1, 2, or 4 cup-size portions. Spoon cooled sauce into freezer containers or jars to within 1 inch of top. Cover and freeze.

To reheat sauce (thaw, if frozen), bring mixture to a simmer over low heat, stirring occasionally. If sauce seems dry, blend in 2 to 4 tablespoons water or dry red wine.

Zucchini Relish

This colorful zucchini relish is crisp and tart. It goes well with any meat or poultry dish.

      5 pounds (about 20 medium-size) zucchini
      6 large onions
          Cold water
      ½ cup salt
      2 cups white wine vinegar
      1 cup sugar
      1 teaspoon dry mustard
      2 teaspoons celery seed
      ½ teaspoon *each* ground cinnamon, nutmeg,
          and pepper
      2 jars (4 oz. *each*) sliced pimentos, drained

Cut zucchini and onions in chunks. Using metal blade, process a portion at a time, with on-off bursts until finely chopped. Place in a 6-quart pan. Cover with water and stir in salt. Cover and refrigerate for 4 hours or overnight.

Drain vegetables, rinse, then drain again. In the same pan combine vegetables, vinegar, sugar, dry mustard, celery seed, cinnamon, nutmeg, pepper, and pimentos. Bring quickly to boiling, stirring constantly. Reduce heat and simmer, uncovered, for about 20 minutes or until mixture is quite thick. Makes 6 pints.

To can relish, fill jars according to directions for Carrot-Orange Marmalade (page 74); then process in a simmering water bath for 15 minutes.

To freeze relish, spoon cooled relish into freezer containers or jars to within 1 inch of the top. Cover and freeze.

Index

Metric Conversion Table

To change	To	Multiply by
ounces (oz.)	grams (g)	28
pounds (lbs.)	kilograms (kg)	0.45
teaspoons	milliliters (ml)	5
tablespoons	milliliters (ml)	15
fluid ounces (fl. oz.)	milliliters (ml)	30
cups	liters (l)	0.24
pints (pt.)	liters (l)	0.47
quarts (qt.)	liters (l)	0.95
gallons (gal.)	liters (l)	3.8
Fahrenheit temperature (°F)	*Celsius temperature (°C)*	*5/9 after subtracting 32*